THE SOCIAL CEO

A Guide to Effective Business Social Media Management

Alberto L. Wilson

DEDICATION

This book is dedicated to those who navigate the dynamic landscape of business leadership with a digital compass. In THE SOCIAL CEO: A Guide to Effective Business Social Media Management, I extend my gratitude to the forward-thinkers who understand that in the interconnected world of today, leadership is not just about vision—it's about conversation.

Here's to the pioneering CEOs who harness the power of social media to foster connections, drive innovation, and lead with authenticity. Your commitment to shaping the future of leadership in the digital age is an inspiration. May this guide serve as a companion on your journey towards social leadership mastery.

ACKNOWLEDGMENT

I am deeply grateful to those whose support and expertise have enriched this endeavor.

First and foremost, I extend my appreciation to my colleagues, whose insightful guidance and unwavering encouragement shaped the narrative of this book.

A heartfelt thank you to my family and friends for their patience, understanding, and constant encouragement throughout this writing journey. Your belief in the significance of this work fueled my determination.

Lastly, my sincere thanks to the readers—CEOs, leaders, and aspiring professionals—whose pursuit of social leadership excellence inspires the purpose of this book.

May THE SOCIAL CEO serve as a guide and catalysts for positive change in the vibrant landscape of business social media management.

PREFACE

I present to you THE SOCIAL CEO: A Guide to Effective Business Social Media Management in the era of interconnectedness, where every post or tweets shapes the narrative of business leadership,

As the boundaries between the corporate and digital worlds blur, this guide emerges as a compass for CEOs navigating the dynamic landscape of social media. It's more than a manual; it's an invitation to explore the transformative power of social engagement in business leadership.

In these pages, we delve into the strategies that transcend traditional boundaries, unlocking the potential for genuine connections, innovation, and meaningful impact. As the author, my aim is to equip you with insights, tools, and guidelines that illuminate the path towards social leadership excellence.

From crafting a compelling online presence to leading through the challenges of real-time communication, THE SOCIAL CEO is a roadmap for leaders or individuals who seek to thrive in the age of digital conversation. As we embark on this journey together, I invite you to embrace the opportunities that social media presents, turning them into instigators for positive change and progressive leadership.

Welcome to a new era of business leadership—a realm where your social presence is as influential as your strategic vision. Let the exploration begin.

TABLE OF CONTENT

THE SOCIAL CEO: A GUIDE TO EFFECTIVE BUSINESS SOCIAL MEDIA MANAGEMENT

BOOK PURPOSE

This book empowers CEOs to take management of their business's social media presence, leading to improved brand awareness, increased engagement, and enhanced business success.

The book includes a 60-day guided exercise and challenge to put your learning and understanding into action. By leveraging the insights and strategies offered in "The Social CEO," you can harness the power of social media to elevate your business and propel it forward.

TARGET AUDIENCE

This handbook is written for CEOs, executives, and business leaders who lack comprehensive knowledge of social media but understand its potential for growth and want to become actively involved in its management.

INTRODUCTION

To trace the evolution of business social media management, we'll embark on a journey that reflects the dynamic landscape of the digital era. The early 2000s witnessed the birth of platforms like LinkedIn and MySpace, establishing the stage for a new era of connectivity. However, it was the advent of Facebook in 2004 and Twitter in 2006 that marked a transformative shift, giving rise to the widespread adoption of social media.

As platforms multiplied and diversified, so did the tools to manage them. The mid-2010s saw the emergence of Instagram and Snapchat, introducing visual content to the social media mix. simultaneously, social media management tools like Hootsuite and TweetDeck were developed to meet the growing needs of businesses, offering centralized platforms for scheduling, analytics, and account management.

In today's digital age, social media has become an indispensable tool for businesses to connect with customers, build brand awareness, and drive sales. And while anyone can post a tweet or create a Facebook page, it takes a special kind of leader to truly leverage the power of social media for business success.

In this groundbreaking book, you'll discover the secrets to becoming a social media-savvy CEO, and how to use your online presence to drive business growth like never before. Packed with actionable tips, easy to follow instructions, and real-world guidelines, this book will show you how to craft a compelling social media strategy that aligns with your business goals, build a strong online presence, and engage with customers in a way that keeps them coming back for more.

Whether you're a seasoned executive looking to take your social media game to the next level, or a new CEO looking to make a splash in the online world, The Social CEO is the ultimate guide to social media success for today's business leaders. So what are you waiting for? Let's dive in and start building your brand today!

Chapter 1

WHY CEO SHOULD BE INVOLVED IN SOCIAL MEDIA

There are several reasons why the CEO should be involved in social media. First, social media is an important tool for building and maintaining the company's online reputation. As the face of the company, the CEO can use social media to showcase their personal brand and communicate the company's values and vision directly to customers, employees, and stakeholders.

Secondly, social media provides a unique opportunity for the CEO to engage with customers and gain valuable insights into their needs and preferences. By actively listening to feedback and engaging in conversations with customers, the CEO can better understand their needs and make informed decisions about the direction of the company.

Thirdly, social media can be an effective tool for driving business growth and increasing sales. By leveraging social media to promote the company's products or services, the CEO can reach a wider audience and attract new customers.

Finally, social media can be used to foster a positive company culture and build employee morale. By sharing company news and milestones on social media, the CEO can demonstrate their commitment to transparency and open communication, which can boost employee engagement and loyalty.

Social media is an important tool for modern business leaders, and the CEO's involvement can have a significant impact on the success of the company.

The Benefits of Social Media for Business

Social media has become an integral part of modern business operations and it has benefits for businesses. Below are some benefits of social media for business;

1. **Increase Brand Awareness**: Social media platforms allow businesses to reach a larger audience and create brand awareness. Businesses can increase their visibility and reach a wider audience by regularly posting engaging content.

2. **Targeted Advertising**: Social media advertising allows businesses to target specific demographics and interests. This enables businesses to reach their ideal customer and increase the likelihood of conversion.

3. **Customer Engagement:** Social media fosters a direct line of communication between businesses and their

customers. This allows businesses to receive feedback, respond to inquiries and build a loyal following.

4. **Cost-Effective Marketing:** Social media marketing can be significantly cheaper than traditional forms of marketing, making it accessible to small and medium-sized businesses.

5. **Improved Customer Insights:** Social media analytics provides businesses with valuable insights into their customer base. This can be used to improve future marketing strategies and product development.

6. **Increased Web Traffic:** Social media can drive traffic to a business's website, increasing their search engine ranking and potentially increasing sales.

Social media provides businesses with a cost-effective and accessible marketing tool, enabling them to increase brand awareness, engage with customers, and drive sales.

The Advantages of CEO Involvement in Social Media

The involvement of CEOs in social media has become increasingly important in today's business landscape. Below are some advantages of CEO involvement in social media:

1. When a CEO actively participates in social media, they can help build the company's brand by providing insights

into the company culture, values, and vision. This can help create a personal connection with customers, employees, and stakeholders.

2. By sharing their expertise and knowledge, CEOs can establish themselves as thought leaders in their industry. This can help build credibility for both the CEO and the company.

3. When CEOs engage with employees on social media, it can help improve enthusiasm and foster a sense of community within the company.

4. In the event of a crisis, having a CEO who is active on social media can be beneficial. They can quickly and effectively communicate with stakeholders, address concerns, and provide updates.

5. CEOs who are active on social media can help attract top talent to the company. By sharing their vision and culture, they can showcase the company's values and mission.

6. Social media can be a valuable tool for monitoring industry trends and staying up-to-date on the latest developments. By actively participating in social media, CEOs can gain insights into what their competitors are doing and stay ahead of the curve.

Chapter 2

SETTING SOCIAL MEDIA GOALS AND STRATEGY

Social media has become an essential tool for businesses to reach their target audience, build brand awareness, and engage with customers. However, to make the most of social media, it's essential to set clear goals and develop a strategy that aligns with those goal and objectives.

Defining your Social Media Goals

Defining social media goals is an important step in creating a successful social media strategy. Here are some steps to help you define your social media goals:

1. Start by identifying what you want to accomplish with your social media efforts. Make sure you goals align with your overall business objectives.
   - ➢ Do you want to increase brand awareness.
   - ➢ Drive traffic to your website.
   - ➢ Generate leads.
   - ➢ Increase sales, or improve customer engagement?

2. **Set measurable goals:** Once you've identified your goals, it's important to make them measurable. This means setting specific targets that you can track and evaluate over time.
   - ➢ For example, if your goal is to increase website traffic, you might set a target of a 20% increase in traffic over the next six months.

3. **Identify your target audience:** Your social media goals should be tailored to your target audience. Determine who your ideal customers are and what social media platforms they use. This will help you create content that resonates with your target audience and achieve your goals more effectively.

4. **Choose the right metrics:** When setting your social media goals, it's important to choose metrics that will help you track progress towards your goals. These could include metrics such as reach, engagement, clicks, conversions, or revenue.

5. **Monitor and adjust:** Keep track of your progress towards your social media goals and adjust your strategy as needed. Use analytics tools to monitor your performance and make changes to your approach if you're not seeing the results you want.

By following these steps, you can identify your target audience and tailor your social media approach to their needs. This will help you build a strong relationship with your customers, increase engagement, and drive business results.

Developing a Social Media Strategy that Aligns with your Business Objective

Developing a social media strategy that aligns with your business objectives is essential to ensure that your social media efforts drive business result. Steps you can follow to develop a social media strategy that aligns with your business objectives:

1. **Define your business objectives:** The first step is to identify your business objectives. What do you want to accomplish with your social media technique? Do you want to increase brand awareness, generate leads, drive website traffic, improve customer service, or increase sales? Once you have a clear understanding of your business objectives, you can create a social media strategy that aligns with them.

2. **Identify your target audience:** Knowing your target audience is crucial in developing an effective social media strategy. Who are your customers? What are their interests, needs, and pain points? Where do they spend their time online? Understanding your target audience will allow you to create content that resonates with them.

3. **Choose the right social media platforms:** Once you know your target audience, you need to choose the social media platforms that they use the most. You don't need to be current on every social media platform. Instead, focus on the ones that are most relevant to your business and your audience.

4. **Develop your content strategy:** Your content strategy should align with your business objectives and target audience. Create content that educates, entertains, or enlightens your audience. Make sure your content is consistent in terms of tone, messaging, and branding.

5. **Plan your content calendar:** Once you have your content strategy, you need to plan your content calendar. Planning a content calendar will help guarantee that you are posting regularly and consistently. Use a content calendar to plan your content in advance and to ensure that your content is relevant to your audience.

6. **Monitor and measure your results:** Finally, it's essential to monitor and measure your results. Use social media analytics tools to track your performance, such as engagement rates, click-through rates, and conversion rates. This will allow you to determine what's working and what's not working so that you can adjust your strategy accordingly.

By following these steps, you can develop a social media strategy that aligns with your business goals and drives results.

Identifying your Target Audience and Tailoring your Social Media Approach to their Needs

Identifying your target audience is very important to developing a successful social media strategy and here are steps you can take to identify your target audience and tailor your social media approach to their needs:

1. **Conduct market research:** Conduct market research to understand who your target audience is, what their interests are, and what motivates them. This can be done through surveys, focus groups, and online analytics tools.

2. **Analyze your existing customer base:** Analyze your existing customer base to understand their demographics, preferences, and behavior. This information can help you identify common characteristics that your target audience shares.

3. **Create customer personas:** Create customer personas to represent your target audience. These personas should include information such as age, gender, location, interests, and behavior patterns.

4. **Tailor your content to their needs:** Once you have identified your target audience, tailor your content to their needs. Create content that addresses their pain points, answers their questions, and provides value to them.

5. **Use the right social media channels:** Choose the right social media channels to reach your target audience. Consider where they spend their time online and what type of content they engage with the most.

6. **Engage with your audience:** Engage with your audience by responding to comments, asking for feedback, and encouraging them to share your content. This will help you build a relationship with your audience and understand their needs better.

7. **Measure your results:** Use social media analytics tools to measure your results and adjust your strategy accordingly. This will help you determine what's working and what's not, and make changes to improve your social media approach.

Exercise: Mastering Social Media for Business Success

Exercise 1: Define Your Social Media Goals

Objective: Set clear and measurable social media goals for your business.

→ List three primary business objectives you aim to achieve through your social media.

→ Define a corresponding social media goal for each business objective. Be specific and ensure alignment.

→ Set measurable targets. For example, if your business goal is to increase sales or improve customer engagement, set a specific percentage increase in social media reach as a target.

→ Reflect on your target audience and ensure your social media goals resonate with their needs and preferences.

→ Choose relevant metrics (e.g., engagement, clicks, conversions) that align with your social media goals.

Exercise 2: Develop Your Social Media Strategy

Objective: Create a comprehensive social media strategy that aligns with your business objectives.

➜ Revisit your identified business objectives and ensure clarity.

➜ Create a detailed characteristics of your target audience, considering demographics, interests, and online behaviors.

➜ Choose the social media platforms that align with your audience's preferences and your business objectives.

➜ Develop a content strategy that aligns with both your business goals and the interests of your target audience. Consider tone, messaging, and branding consistency.

➜ Create a content calendar to plan and organize your social media posts. Ensure regular and consistent posting aligned with your strategy.

➜ Identify key performance indicators (KPIs) and set up a system for monitoring, measuring results and also establish a schedule for reviewing and adjusting your strategy based on performance.

Exercise 3: Identify Your Target Audience and Tailor Your Approach

Objective: Understand and connect with your target audience.

→ Outline the steps you will take to conduct market research, including surveys, focus groups, and online analytics tools.

→ List ways to analyze your existing customer base, understanding their demographics, preferences, and behaviors.

→ Create a well detailed customer personas representing different segments of your target audience

→ Outline strategies to tailor your content to address the needs and interests of your identified target audience.

→ Consider where your target audience spends time online and choose the most relevant social media channels for engagement.

→ Develop a plan for engaging with your audience through comments, feedback, and content sharing. Identify metrics for measuring the effectiveness of your engagement strategies.

Regularly revisit and adjust your social media goals and strategies based on ongoing analysis and changing business needs.

Chapter 3

CHOOSING THE RIGHT SOCIAL MEDIA PLATFORMS

Choosing the right social media platforms for your business is an essential step in developing a successful social media marketing strategy.

Overview of Major Social Media Platforms

1. **Facebook:** Facebook is the largest social media platform in the world, with over 2.8 billion monthly active users. It allows users to connect with friends and family, join groups, share photos and videos, and follow pages.

2. **Instagram:** Instagram is a photo and video sharing app owned by Facebook. It has over 1.2 billion monthly active users and is particularly popular among younger generations. Instagram features include filters, Stories, Reels, and IGTV.

3. **Twitter:** Twitter is a microblogging platform with over 330 million monthly active users. Users can share short messages or "tweets," follow accounts, and participate in conversations through hashtags.

4. **LinkedIn:** LinkedIn is a professional networking platform with over 740 million members. It allows users to create a professional profile, connect with other professionals, and search for job opportunities.

5. **YouTube:** YouTube is a video sharing platform with over 2 billion monthly active users. It allows users to upload and watch videos on a wide range of topics, from music and entertainment to educational and informative content.

6. **TikTok**: TikTok is a short-form video sharing app with over 1 billion monthly active users. It allows users to create and share 15-60 second videos, often set to music or other audio.

There are many other social media platforms, but these are some of the most popular and widely used ones.

How to Choose the Best Platforms for your Business

> The first step is to identify your target audience and their preferred social media platforms. Different platforms appeal to different demographics, so research your audience to find out where they spend their time online.

➤ **Consider your business type:** Certain social media platforms are better suited for specific types of businesses. For example, LinkedIn is a great platform for B2B companies, while Instagram is ideal for businesses that are visually appealing such as fashion, food or travel.

➤ Decide what you want to achieve with your social media marketing. Do you want to increase brand awareness, drive traffic to your website, generate leads or build customer relationships? Each platform has its strengths, so choose the one(s) that align with your goals.

➤ Consider the time, budget, and expertise required to effectively manage each platform. If you have limited resources, it's better to focus on a few platforms rather than trying to be present on every social media site.

➤ **Keep an eye on the competition:** See which social media platforms your competitors are using and how they are leveraging them. This can provide insight into where you should focus your efforts.

➤ Once you have selected your platforms, test your strategies and measure your results. This will help you determine what works and what doesn't and make adjustments accordingly.

Choosing the right social media platforms for your business takes time and research. By understanding your target audience, business goals, available resources, and competition, you can make informed decisions about which platforms to use to achieve your marketing objectives.

Understanding Platform-Specific Nuances and Optimizing Content Accordingly

Understanding platform-specific nuances and optimizing content simply means tailoring your social media content to match the unique characteristics, features, and user behaviors of each social media platform. Each platform has its own strengths, audience preferences, and content formats. Optimizing your content for each social media platform can help you maximize engagement and reach. Below are some platform-specific nuances to keep in mind:

1. Facebook: Facebook is a great platform to build a community around your brand and engage with your audience through conversations and comments.

> ➤ To optimize your content on Facebook, focus on creating shareable and interactive posts, such as polls, questions, or user-generated content.
> ➤ Consider using Facebook Live to broadcast events or behind-the-scenes content.

2. Instagram: Instagram is a highly visual platform, where aesthetics and creativity matter.

> ➤ To optimize your content on Instagram, use high-quality photos or videos, and leverage the power of storytelling through captions, hashtags, and Stories.

➢ You can also experiment with different formats, such as Reels or IGTV, to showcase your brand personality and engage with your followers.

3. Twitter: Twitter is a fast-paced platform that thrives on real-time conversations and trending topics.
➢ To optimize your content on Twitter, use short and catchy tweets, reply to mentions and direct messages promptly, and leverage hashtags to join relevant conversations.
➢ Use Twitter's multimedia features, such as polls, GIFs, or videos, to make your content more engaging.

4. LinkedIn: LinkedIn is a professional platform that focuses on networking, thought leadership, and career development.
➢ To optimize your content on LinkedIn, create informative/insightful articles, share industry news/trends, and highlight your expertise through testimonials and case studies.
➢ Also, use LinkedIn's publishing platform to reach a wider audience and establish yourself as a thought leader in your field.

5. YouTube: YouTube is a video-centric platform that offers a wide range of content formats and niches.
➢ To optimize your content on YouTube, create informative and entertaining videos.
➢ Use eye-catching thumbnails and titles.
➢ Leverage YouTube's SEO features to rank higher in search results.

➢ Use YouTube's community features, such as comments, live streams, or collaborations, to engage with your viewers and grow your channel.

Each social media platform has its own audience, culture, and algorithm, so optimizing your content accordingly can help you stand out and achieve your goals.

Chapter 4

SETTING UP AND OPTIMIZING YOUR SOCIAL MEDIA PROFILES

Setting up and optimizing your social media profiles involves creating a strong online presence for yourself or your business on social media platforms.

Creating a Consistent Brand Image

Creating a consistent brand image is crucial for building a strong brand identity that resonates with your target audience. Here are some guidelines for creating a consistent brand image:

1. Develop a clear brand strategy that outlines your brand values, personality, and positioning. This is the foundation for creating a consistent brand image.

2. **Use a consistent brand voice:** Your brand voice is the tone and style of your communication. Whether it's on social media, website or email marketing, make sure your brand voice is consistent and recognizable.

3. **Create brand guidelines:** Brand guidelines provide a set of rules for how your brand should be represented. It covers everything from logo usage to color palette to typography. A comprehensive brand guideline ensures consistency in your brand image.

4. **Use consistent visual elements:** Visual elements such as color, font, and imagery should be consistent across all brand materials. Consistent visual elements can help your brand be more memorable and recognizable.

5. **Maintain consistency across all channels:** Whether it's your website, social media platforms, or offline materials, maintaining consistency across all channels is important. It helps to create a unified brand image that customers can easily recognize.

By following these guidelines, you can create a consistent brand image that strengthens your brand identity and helps to build trust and loyalty with your audience.

Writing Compelling Profile Descriptions and Headlines

Writing a compelling profile description and headline is very important when it comes to attracting potential readers or customers.

1. **Know your target audience:** Understanding your target audience is essential when it comes to crafting a compelling profile description and headline. Consider the

age, interests, and values of your audience and tailor your language and tone accordingly.

2. **Highlight your unique selling proposition:** What makes you or your product/service different from others? Highlighting your unique selling proposition in your headline and profile description will help you stand out from the competition.

3. **Use persuasive language:** Use persuasive language to encourage readers to engage with your profile or click through to your website. Use action words and strong verbs to create a sense of urgency and excitement.

4. **Keep it concise:** Keep your headline and profile description brief and to the point. Use short sentences and avoid unnecessary information. Remember that you want to capture your audience's attention quickly.

5. **Incorporate keywords:** Incorporating keywords related to your industry or niche can help improve your search engine rankings and attract relevant readers.

6. **Include social proof:** Including social proof, such as customer reviews or testimonials, can help establish credibility and build trust with potential customers.

7. Make sure to update your profile description and headline regularly to keep it fresh and relevant. This can also help improve your search engine rankings and keep readers engaged.

Choosing Profile and Cover Photos

Choosing profile and cover photos can be an important aspect of presenting yourself on social media or other online platforms and below are some tips to consider when selecting your profile and cover photos:

➢ Choose a clear and high-quality image.
➢ Use a photo that represents you or your brand.
➢ Keep it simple.
➢ Consider the size and layout of the photos.
➢ Be mindful of copyright

1. **Choose a clear and high-quality image:** Make sure that your profile and cover photos are clear and of high quality. Avoid blurry or pixelated images that can detract from your online presence.

2. **Use a photo that represents you or your brand:** Your profile and cover photos should reflect your personal or professional brand. Use images that are consistent with your message or values.

3. **Keep it simple:** Avoid cluttered or busy images that can be distracting. Choose simple, straightforward images that are easy to understand and resonate with your audience.

4. **Consider the size and layout of the photos:** Make sure that your profile and cover photos are sized and cropped correctly for the platform you are using. Check the

dimensions and resolution requirements to ensure that your photos look their best.

5. **Be mindful of copyright:** Only use images that you have the rights to use. Avoid using copyrighted images without permission.

Using Keywords and Hashtags

Both keywords and hashtags can help people find your content, but they serve different purposes and work in different ways. Below is a breakdown of keywords and hashtags.

Keywords:

➢ Used for search engines like Google and Bing.
➢ It's purpose is to help users find specific information through targeted searches.
➢ It is usually incorporated organically within content (text, titles,descriptions).
➢ Can be very specific, targeting long-tail queries and niche searches.
➢ Competition is high, as many businesses compete for the same keywords.
➢ **Example:** If you write a blog post about "vegan leather shoes for men," relevant keywords might be *"vegan men's shoes," or "eco-friendly footwear,"* e.t.c.

Hashtags:

➢ Used for Social media platforms like Instagram, Twitter, and TikTok.

- It's purpose is to categorize and discover content within the platform based on user-generated tags.
- It is preceded by a pound sign (#) and added to captions or bios.
- It can be general or specific, depending on the topic and platform.
- Competition varies depending on the popularity of the hashtag.
- **Example:** For the same blog post about vegan leather shoes for men, relevant hashtags might be *#veganshoes, #mensfashion or #ecofriendlyliving.*

Tips for using keywords and hashtags effectively:

1. **Research relevant keywords and hashtags:** Do some research to find out what keywords and hashtags are commonly used in your industry or niche. Look at what your competitors are using.

Let your targeted keywords and hashtags be relevant to your content and audience. Using generic terms can lead to lower discoverability.

Use tools like Google Keyword Planner or Hashtagify to find relevant keywords and hashtags.

2. **Use keywords in your profile and content:** Use relevant keywords in your profile bio and in the content that you post. This will help your content to show up in search

results when people are looking for information related to those keywords.

3. Use relevant hashtags in your posts to increase visibility and engagement. Hashtags help your content to show up in searches and also make it easier for people to find and follow your content.

4. Use a mix of popular and niche hashtags as it can help you reach a wider audience while also targeting specific niche communities.

Below are some examples of popular and niche hashtags for different types of content, platforms, and industries:

Platform

Instagram:
→ Popular: #love, #food, #photooftheday, #fashion, #travel
→ Niche: #veganfoodie, #smallbusiness, #bookstagram, #wanderlust, #sustainableliving

Twitter:
→ Popular: #news, #politics, #sports, #memes.
→ Niche: #codinglife, #arttherapy, #productivityhacks, #cryptocurrency

LinkedIn:
→ Popular: #careers, #networking, #leadership, #jobs #entrepreneur.
→ Niche: #remotework, #dataanalysis, #contentmarketing, #womenintech, #digitalmarketing, #fintech

---

Industry

Fashion:
→ Popular: #fashionblogger, #style, #shoes, #dress
→ Niche: #slowfashion, #vintageclothing, #ethicalfashion, #plussizefashion, #menswear, #readytowearfashion

Food:
→ Popular:#foodie, #cooking, #baking, #foodphotography, #dinner
→ Niche: #veganrecipes, #healthylifestyle, #ketodiet, #plantbasediet #foodstyling, #glutenfree

Travel:
→ Popular: #travelgram, #wanderlust, #adventure, #photography, #explore
→ Niche: #solotravel, #budgettravel, #backpacking, #sustainabletravel

Content Type

Blog post:
→ Popular: #tips, #howto, #advice, #guide, #lifehacks
→ Niche: #mentalhealth, #finance #digitalmarketing, #freelancing, #investing, #personaldevelopment

Video:
→ Popular:#comedy, #music, #motivation, #gaming, #vlog
→ Niche: #animation, #documentary, #educational, #historical, #diy

5. Don't overuse hashtags or use irrelevant hashtags just to get more visibility. Make sure that the hashtags you use are relevant to your content and your audience.

Using keywords and hashtags is just one part of a successful social media or online marketing strategy. It's important to also focus on creating high-quality content and engaging with your audience to build relationships and grow your followers.

<u>Tools for Researching Keywords and Hashtags</u>

Keyword Research:

➢ Google Keyword Planner.
➢ SEMrush Keyword Magic Tool.
➢ Ahrefs Keywords Explorer.
➢ Moz Keyword Explorer.
➢ AnswerthePublic.

➢ **Google Keyword Planner** is a free tool by Google and it is ideal for understanding search volume and competition for keywords.

➢ **SEMrush Keyword Magic Tool** is a paid tool offering deep insights into keyword trends, related keywords, and competitor analysis.

➢ **Ahrefs Keywords Explorer** is similar to SEMrush and It provides comprehensive keyword data and competitor analysis.

➢ **Moz Keyword Explorer** offers keyword suggestions, difficulty scores, and opportunities for long-tail keywords.

➢ **AnswerthePublic** generates question-based keywords based on user searches.

Hashtag Research:

- Hashtagify.me.
- RiteTag.
- Trends24.
- Keyhole.
- Sprout Social.

- **Hashtagify.me** analyzes hashtag popularity, influencer usage and related hashtags.

- **RiteTag** suggests relevant hashtags based on your content and also analyzes potential reach and engagement.

- **Trends24** tracks trending hashtags on Twitter and other platforms in real-time.

- **Keyhole** provides historical and real-time hashtag analytics across social media platforms.

- **Sprout Social** offers comprehensive social media analytics, including hashtag performance tracking.

Tools for Analyzing Performance and Staying Updated on Trending Topics

Performance Analysis:

- Google Analytics.
- Social media platform analytics.
- Brand24.
- Buzzsumo, and Sprout Social.

➢ **Google Analytics** tracks website traffic and user behavior, including keyword referrals and hashtag performance.

➢ **Social media platform analytics:** Each platform offers built-in analytics tools to track post performance, including engagement and hashtag reach.

➢ **Brand24** monitors brand mentions and analyzes sentiment across social media, news, and blogs.

➢ **Buzzsumo** analyzes content performance and identifies trending topics across various platforms.

➢ **Sprout Social** is similar to Brand24 and it tracks brand mentions and analyzes sentiment across multiple channels.

Staying Updated on Trends:

➢ Google Trends (trends.google.com)
➢ Twitter Trends.
➢ Social media platform trend lists.
➢ Industry blogs and publications
➢ Influencer accounts

➢ **Google Trends** tracks trending search topics globally and regionally.

➢ **Twitter Trends** shows live trending topics on Twitter based on location and interests.

➢ **Social media platform trend lists:** Each platform often highlights trending topics and hashtags within its interface.

➢ Stay informed about trends and news by following relevant blogs and publications within your field.

➢ Follow key influencers in your industry to see what topics and hashtags they are using.

The best tools depend on your specific needs and budget. Don't hesitate to try various options and experiment until you find a combination that works for you!

Chapter 5

DEVELOPING A CONTENT STRATEGY

Developing a content strategy is like creating the roadmap for your online presence. It is an important part of creating a successful online presence and below are tips for developing a content strategy:

1. Identify your goals: Setting goals is the first stage in creating a content strategy. Your content strategy should be in line with the objectives of your entire organization.
   ➢ Do you want to enhance revenue, lead generation, or brand awareness?

2. Identify your target audience: Your content should be tailored to your target audience. Understanding your target audience is key to creating content that resonates with them.
   ➢ Who are they?
   ➢ What are their interests, pain points, and needs?

3. Pick the formats for your content: Think about the formats that will help you reach your target audience and accomplish your objectives.

> ➢ What kinds of content are you going to produce?
> ➢ Will you prioritize podcasts, infographics, videos, social media posts, or blog pieces?

4. Develop a content calendar: You can plan and arrange your content using a content calendar. Topics, formats, distribution methods, and publication dates are all possible. Be mindful to schedule your content in advance and adhere to it consistently.

5. Optimize your content for search engines: SEO (Search Engine Optimization) is important for getting your content found by your target audience. Use relevant keywords in your content, optimize your meta descriptions and tags, and make sure your website is mobile-friendly and fast-loading.

6. Measure and analyze your results: Measuring the performance of your content is essential for optimizing your content strategy. Use analytics tools to track your website traffic, engagement, and conversion rates. Use this data to adjust and improve your content strategy.

Consistently creating high-quality content that resonates with your target audience is key to building a strong online presence and achieving your business goals.

Creating a Content Calendar

A content calendar is a mechanism that helps to plan and manage your content in advance. Here are the steps to create a content calendar:

1. **Define your content themes:** Start by identifying the themes that your content will focus on. These could be topics related to your industry, products or services, or any other areas that are relevant to your target audience.

2. **Determine your posting frequency:** Decide how often you will be posting content, and on which social media platforms. This will help you plan out the number of posts you need to create for each platform.

3. **Choose your content types:** Choose the types of content you will be creating, such as blog posts, videos, infographics, or social media posts. Consider the content types that are most effective for reaching your target audience and achieving your goals.

4. **Set deadlines:** Assign deadlines for each piece of content you plan to create. This will help you stay on track and ensure that you have enough time to create and edit each piece of content.

5. **Plan out your content:** Use a calendar tool to plan out your content. You can use a spreadsheet or a dedicated content calendar tool. Decide on the specific topics for

each piece of content, and assign them to specific dates and times.

6. **Review and adjust your calendar:** Regularly review and adjust your content calendar based on feedback from your audience, changes in your business, and performance metrics. This will help you refine your content strategy and improve the effectiveness of your content.

By following these steps, you can create a content calendar that helps you stay organized, consistent, and strategic in your content creation.

Determining the Frequency and Timing of Posts

Determining the frequency and timing of posts is an important part of creating a successful social media strategy. Here are some tips for deciding on the frequency and timing of your social media posts:

1. **Understand your audience:** Knowing your target audience is key to determining the best frequency and timing for your posts. Consider when your audience is most active on social media and how often they like to see new content.

2. **Be consistent:** Consistency is important when it comes to social media. Consistency helps build brand awareness and engagement. You can create a schedule that you can stick to over the long term.

3. **Determine the ideal posting frequency:** The ideal posting frequency will depend on the social media platforms you're using and the preferences of your target audience. Generally, you should aim to post on each platform at least once a day, but you may need to adjust your posting frequency based on your audience's preferences.

4. **Test and measure:** Test different posting frequencies and track your engagement metrics. Use this data to adjust your posting schedule and determine what works best for your audience.

5. **Consider the best times to post:** There are certain times when social media users are most active. Consider posting during peak times to maximize your reach and engagement. For example, on Instagram, the best time to post is generally between 11 am and 1 pm during weekdays.

6. **Use scheduling tools:** Scheduling tools can help you plan and schedule your posts in advance. This can save you time and ensure that your posts are published at the right time.

The frequency and timing of your posts will depend on your audience, your goals, and the social media platforms you're using.

By staying consistent and strategic with your social media posts, you can build a strong online presence and achieve your business goals.

Types of Content to Consider

(e.g., images, videos, blog posts, etc.)

There are many types of content that you can create and share on social media. Here are some of the most popular types of content to consider:

1. **Images:** Images are one of the most common types of content on social media. They can be photos or graphics that help to visually communicate your brand, products, or services.

2. **Videos:** Videos can be a highly engaging and shareable form of content. They can be used to showcase your products, share tutorials or tips, or tell stories about your brand.

3. **Blog posts:** Blog posts can be shared on social media to drive traffic to your website and establish thought leadership in your industry. They can be used to share insights, industry news, and tips or how-tos.

4. **Infographics:** Infographics are a visually appealing way to share data and statistics. They can be used to educate your audience on complex topics or to highlight industry trends.

5. **User-generated content:** User-generated content (UGC) is content created by your audience, such as customer reviews, photos, or videos. UGC can be a powerful way to

build brand loyalty and showcase your products or services.

6. **Polls and surveys:** Polls and surveys can be used to engage your audience and gather valuable feedback on your products or services.

7. **Live videos:** Live videos allow you to connect with your audience in real-time. You can use live videos to host Q&A sessions, product demos, or to give behind-the-scenes glimpses of your business.

8. **Podcasts:** Podcasts can be a valuable form of content for reaching audiences that prefer audio content. They can be used to share insights, industry news, or interviews with experts.

When creating your social media content strategy, consider the types of content that resonate with your audience and help you achieve your goals.

Chapter 6

CRAFTING ENGAGING SOCIAL MEDIA CONTENT

Crafting engaging social media content is the process of creating posts, videos, and other materials that capture the attention of your target audience, encourage interaction, and build a loyal followers on social media platforms. It involves going beyond just promoting your brand or product and providing genuine value and entertainment for your viewers.

Crafting engaging social media content requires a combination of creativity, strategy, and understanding of your target audience and below are some key aspects of crafting engaging social media content:

1. Understand your audience.

➢ Who are you trying to reach? Know their demographics, interests, and online behavior and tailor your content to their preferences.

➢ What are their pain points and aspirations? Address their needs and offer solutions they care about.

➤ What platforms do they frequent? Adapt your content format and voice to each platform's unique characteristics.

2. Focus on value and engagement.

➤ Offer valuable insights, tips, and behind-the-scenes glimpses to keep your audience interested. ***Don't just sell. Educate and entertain.***

➤ Encourage comments, shares, and polls to foster a sense of community. ***Ask questions and spark conversations.***

➤ Run contests and giveaways. Incentivize participation and attract new followers.

3. Variety is key.

➤ Experiment with different content formats by creating engaging visuals like photos, videos, infographics, and live streams to keep your audience scrolling.

➤ Share personal experiences, anecdotes, and company culture to build a stronger connection with your audience.

➤ Respond to current events, trending topics, and holidays to demonstrate your brand's awareness and connection to the world.

4. Optimize for visibility.

➤ Research popular and niche hashtags your target audience is likely to use. ***Use relevant hashtags.***

➢ Include catchy captions and calls to action. Tell them what you want them to do, whether it's visiting your website, engaging with your post or subscribing to your channel.

➢ Post consistently and strategically. Stick to a regular posting schedule and consider peak times on each platform to maximize reach.

5. Analyzing and adapting.

➢ Track your performance by using analytics tools to see what content resonates most, what platforms deliver the best results, and what times generate the most engagement.

➢ Be open to feedback and adapt your strategy. Learn from your audience's reactions and iterate your content based on their preferences.

Crafting engaging social media content is an ongoing process and by consistently applying these principles and analyzing your results, you can create a strong online presence that attracts and retains your target audience, achieves your brand goals, and fosters meaningful connections.

Guides to Creating Compelling Content

1. Know who your audience is, what they like, what interests them, and what kind of content they engage with the most.

2. Use high-quality images, videos, and graphics that grab attention and communicate your message effectively.

3. Social media users have a short attention span, so keep your content concise and to the point.

4. **Use humor:** Humor is a great way to engage with your audience and make your content more memorable.

5. Use storytelling to create an emotional connection with your audience and to make your content more relatable. Storytelling is the art of conveying a narrative through the use of words, images, or other forms of communication. It involves the creation and sharing of stories, often with the goal of entertaining, educating, or persuading an audience.

6. Provide value to your audience by sharing useful tips, insights, and information.

7. Use relevant hashtags to make your content more discoverable and to connect with like-minded individuals.

8. Respond to comments, messages, and mentions to build relationships with your audience and create a sense of community.

9. Experiment with different formats by trying out different formats such as polls, quizzes, and interactive content to keep your audience engaged and interested.

10. Post regularly and consistently to maintain a strong presence on social media and to keep your audience engaged.

Actionable Steps for Crafting Engaging Content

1. Understand Your Audience.

Actionable steps:

→ Create customer personas by defining your ideal audience profiles with demographics, interests, online behavior, and pain points. **(Tools; Xtensio, HubSpot's MakeMyPersona)**

→ Analyze existing audience data by utilizing platform analytics (e.g., Facebook Insights, Twitter Analytics) to understand demographics, content engagement, and popular topics.

→ Conduct surveys and polls: Ask your audience directly about their preferences, challenges, and social media habits. **(Tools; SurveyMonkey or Google Forms)**

Resources:

→ Tools like Brand24 or Meltwater can track online conversations and identify trends surrounding your brand and industry.

→ Industry reports and studies can provide broader insights into your target audience's characteristics and online behavior.

2. Focus on Value and Engagement.

Actionable steps:

→ Share actionable advice, industry news, or educational content related to your audience's interests.

→ Run interactive campaigns by using polls, quizzes, contests, or live Q&A sessions to encourage participation and spark conversations.

→ Partner with relevant influencers to reach new audiences and gain access to their expertise.

Resources:

→ Plan out your content in advance with diverse formats like blog posts, infographics, and videos. **(Tools; Hootsuite or Sprout Social)**

→ Leverage features like pinned comments, stories polls, or live video to boost interaction.

→ Influencer marketing platforms: Tools like HypeAuditor or Buzzsumo can help identify relevant influencers and track their audience demographics and engagement.

3. Variety is Key.

Actionable steps:

→ Experiment with different content formats by utilizing image/video carousels, short-form videos (TikTok, Reels), behind-the-scenes glimpses, or user-generated content.

→ Share inspiring customer experiences, brand origin stories, or relatable anecdotes to connect with your audience on an emotional level.

→ Keep your content relevant by incorporating timely topics and discussions into your posts.

Resources:

→ Tools like Canva or Lumen5 offer templates and easy-to-use features for creating visuals and videos.

→ Books and online courses on storytelling techniques can help you craft compelling narratives for your content.

4. Optimize for Visibility.

Actionable steps:

→ Use a combination of popular and niche hashtags your target audience is likely to search for. **(Tools; Hashtagify.me or RiteTag).**

→ Craft engaging captions that summarize your content, include relevant keywords, and encourage action.

→ Publish strategically by posting when your audience is most active on each platform. **(Tool; Sprout Social offer optimal posting times suggestions).**

Resources:

→ Schedule your posts in advance and across multiple platforms for consistency and optimal reach.

→ Track your content performance to understand which posts resonate most and identify areas for improvement.

5. Analyzing and Adapting:

Actionable steps:

→ Monitor engagement metrics like likes, shares, comments, and reach to analyze content performance.

→ Respond to comments and messages, conduct surveys, and actively seek feedback to understand what works and what doesn't work.

→ Analyze your results and refine your content style, format, and posting schedule based on what resonates with your audience.

Resources:

> → Tools like Sprout Social or Hootsuite offer A/B testing features to compare different content variations and identify the best performing ones.
>
> → Join online communities or forums specific to your industry or target audience to gain insights and feedback from other users and professionals.

The (4) Actions

The (4) Actions and how each Contributes to Building a Loyal Following. While all four actions contribute to building a loyal following, each of them plays a distinct role in the process.

- ➢ Likes.
- ➢ Shares.
- ➢ Comments.
- ➢ Brand mentions.

Likes are quick and simple indication of appreciation for your content.

- ➢ Likes Increases visibility. It can trigger algorithms to prioritize your content in users' feeds, potentially exposing it to more people.

- ➢ A high number of likes can act as a validation tool, encouraging others to engage with your content.

➢ While not explicit, likes can indicate general positive sentiment towards your brand or content.

Shares are actively distributing your content to the networks of a follower and expanding reach exponentially.

➢ Shares have the potential to propel your content to a wider audience beyond your followers, fostering organic reach and brand awareness.

➢ Sharing signifies a higher level of engagement and advocacy, demonstrating that your content resonates with some followers.

➢ Shared content sparks conversations within the follower's network, encouraging interaction and potentially attracting new followers.

Comments are two-way interaction where followers offer their thoughts, questions, or opinions on your content.

➢ Comments indicate deeper engagement and a willingness to interact directly with your brand.

➢ Comments provide valuable feedback on your content and brand perception, aiding in improvement and building stronger connections.

➢ Comments boost reach. Platforms may prioritize content with high comment activity, increasing organic reach within existing followers.

Brand Mentions are any reference to your brand in another user's content, even without tagging your account.

➢ Mentions give you organic reach and awareness.

➢ Mentions expose your brand to new audiences beyond your followers, expanding reach and sparking curiosity.

➢ Tracking brand mentions reveals valuable insights into audience sentiment and perception, aiding in strategy refinement.

➢ Mentions build authenticity. Organic mentions suggest your brand resonates beyond your curated platforms, indicating genuine popularity and trust.

While each action has its own value and potential, the real magic lies in their combined effect. A post with high likes, shares, and comments creates a buzz, attracting more attention and organic engagement. Brand mentions then amplify the reach. This positive cycle fosters audience trust and loyalty, solidifying your brand image and attracting new followers.

Encourage followers to like, comment and share your content.

Respond to comments and mentions to build relationships and show appreciation for audience interaction.

Crafting Post that Spark Conversations

1. Ask intriguing questions: Go beyond "What do you think?" with open-ended, thought-provoking inquiries that tap into your audience's interests and opinions. For example;

> ➤ **Questions that challenge perceptions (i.e;** "What historical event do you think should be taught in schools that isn't currently included?")

> ➤ **Questions that ignite creativity (i.e;** "Describe your ideal day using only emojis.")

> ➤ **Questions that foster empathy and connection (i.e;** "Share an act of kindness you witnessed recently that brightened your day.")

> ➤ **Questions that spark debate and discussion (i.e;** "Is artificial intelligence(A.I) a threat or a tool for human progress?")

> ➤ **Questions that encourage personal reflection (i.e;** "What is one skill you wish you could master with zero effort?")

- *Tailor your questions to your audience and brand identity.*
- *Keep them concise and easy to understand.*

- *Use engaging visuals or video along with your questions to grab attention.*
- *Respond to comments and participate in the discussion you generated.*

Keep in mind that the goal is to go beyond basic opinions and inspire genuine thought and conversation. So, by asking intriguing questions that challenge assumptions, ignite creativity, and spark meaningful connections, you can turn your social media platforms into vibrant communities where your audience feels heard, engaged and valued.

2. Share relatable anecdotes: Personal stories or relatable experiences can spark shared feelings and encourage others to chime in with their own thoughts.

3. Run polls and quizzes: Interactive elements like polls and quizzes not only gather information but it can also encourage healthy competition and discussion.

4. Host live Q&A sessions: Offer direct interaction and answer your audience questions in real-time. It will help foster a sense of community and engagement.

5. Tag relevant individuals or brands: Engage other accounts in your field to broaden the conversation and attract their followers.

Crafting Post that Spark Collaboration

1. Pose design challenges or creative prompts: Spark community creativity by inviting collaboration on recipes, artwork, or stories related to your brand.

2. Run hashtag contests: Encourage user-generated content with specific hashtags and showcase winning entries to highlight audience contributions.

3. Collaborate with relevant influencers or brands to combine audiences and also generate cross-promotion opportunities.

4. Reward your followers with unique experiences or content for participating in collaborative activities.

5. Ask for feedback and ideas: Actively invite your audience to contribute their thoughts and suggestions. It will demonstrate your openness to collaboration.

Crafting Post that Spark Website Visits

1. Share valuable blog posts, articles, or guide with clear call to action directing users to your website for the full experience.

2. Showcase compelling visuals and teasers that pique curiosity and entice users to click through to learn more.

3. Run limited-time website offers or promotions: create urgency and exclusivity with special deals or discounts available only through your website.

4. Utilize website link snippets: Platforms like Instagram Stories or Twitter bios offer dedicated spaces to display your website link prominently.

5. Make your bio and captions are SEO-friendly: Include relevant keywords in your bio and captions to increase organic discoverability when users search for related topics.

Understanding the Importance of Visual Content

Visual content is any type of media that conveys information or communicates a message through images or video. This includes photographs, illustrations, infographics, animations, videos, and other visual aids.

Visual content is incredibly important in today's digital landscape. Here are a few reasons why visual content is important:

1. **Grabs Attention:** Visual content, such as images and videos, immediately capture people's attention, especially in a world where we are bombarded with information every second.

2. **Memorable**: Visual content is more memorable than text-based content. Studies have shown that people remember visual content better than text.

3. **Increases Engagement:** Visual content can increase engagement with your audience. Social media platforms,

for example, are dominated by visual content because it generates more likes, shares, and comments.

4. **Helps to Convey Information:** Visual content is an effective way to convey complex information. For example, infographics can communicate data and statistics in an easy-to-understand format.

5. **Builds Brand Identity:** Visual content is an excellent way to build brand identity. Using consistent visual elements such as colors, fonts, and imagery can help your brand become recognizable and stand out in a crowded marketplace.

Creating Compelling Visual Content

Creating compelling visual content involves several key steps which include the following;

➢ Identify the goal of your visual content. Whether it's to inform, entertain, or inspire. Knowing your purpose will help guide your design.

➢ Understand your target audience's preferences, interests, visual style and tailor your design to resonate with them.

➢ Consider where your visual content will be shared. Each platform may have different requirements and best practices. So, it's best you choose the right platform.

➤ Clearly define the message you want to convey. Keep it concise and focused to avoid overwhelming or confusing your audience.

➤ Select engaging visual elements by using high-quality images, graphics, or illustrations that align with your message. Ensure they are visually appealing and relevant.

➤ Maintain consistency with your brand colors, fonts, and logo as this will helps establish a cohesive and recognizable visual identity.

➤ Arrange visual elements in a balanced and aesthetically pleasing manner. Pay attention to spacing, hierarchy, and overall composition.

➤ Be mindful of color psychology. Use colors wisely by choosing a color scheme that complements your brand and elicits the desired emotions.

➤ Select fonts that enhance readability and match your brand personality. For instance, use different font sizes to emphasize key points.

➤ Encourage engagement by including a clear and compelling call to action. Whether it's to visit a website or share the content.

➤ Optimize for mobile by ensuring your visual content is mobile-friendly. Many users access content on smartphones, so optimize for various screen sizes.

➤ Before finalizing, gather feedback and test your visual content. Iterate based on insights to improve its effectiveness.

➤ Respect copyright and licensing laws when using images or content. Be careful and ensure you have the right to use and modify any elements in your design.

➤ Check for errors, typos, or any inconsistencies. A polished and error-free design reflects professionalism.

➤ Save your visual content in the right and appropriate format for the intended use, whether it's a JPEG, PNG, GIF, or other formats.

Chapter 7

BUILDING A STRONG ONLINE COMMUNITY

Building a strong online community means creating a group of individuals who share a common interest or passion and who interact with each other online regularly. This community can be built around a brand, product, or service, and it's essential for businesses and organizations that want to create a loyal following and engage with their audience in a meaningful way.

Advantages of Building a Strong Online Community

Advantages of Building a Strong Online Community around your Brand;

1. **Increased customer loyalty**: An online community provides a space where customers can engage with your brand, share feedback, and connect with like-minded individuals. This can help to build a sense of loyalty among your customer base, as they feel they are part of a larger community.

Create a loyal customer base by providing a space for engagement, feedback, and connection within a larger community.

2. **Improved customer support**: An online community can serve as a platform for customers to ask questions, seek advice, and receive support from both your brand and other community members. This can reduce the workload on your customer support team and provide a more efficient and personalized service.

3. **Valuable feedback**: By engaging with your customers in an online community, you can gain valuable insights into their needs, preferences, and pain points. This feedback can help you to improve your products or services and make better-informed business decisions.

4. **Increased brand awareness**: An online community can help to increase brand awareness and attract new customers. When members of the community share their positive experiences with others, it can lead to word-of-mouth marketing and a wider reach for your brand.

5. **Opportunities for collaboration:** Building an online community can create opportunities for collaboration with other businesses or organizations. By partnering with like-minded brands or individuals, you can expand your reach and create new opportunities for growth.

Strategies for Fostering Engagement and Interaction

Fostering engagement and interaction is essential for creating a positive and productive environment in any setting, whether it's a workplace, a classroom, or an online community. Here are some tips for fostering engagement and interaction

1. **Create a welcoming environment:** Make sure people feel welcome and included. Encourage everyone to participate and respect diverse opinions.

For instance, start each session with a warm welcome message, encouraging members to share a brief introduction.

---

2. **Use icebreakers:** Start with a fun and easy activity to get everyone comfortable and interacting. It could be as simple as introducing yourself or sharing a fun fact.

3. **Encourage questions**: Invite people to ask questions and offer answers. This promotes an interactive environment and helps everyone learn.

For instance, begin discussions with an 'Ask Me Anything' segment to foster curiosity and active participation.

---

4. **Use visual aids:** Visual aids like videos, pictures, and charts can make your content more engaging and help people understand concepts better.

For instance, share an infographic summarizing key points before a discussion to enable understanding and engagement.

5. **Break up presentations**: Instead of a long presentation, break it up with interactive activities or discussions. This will keep people engaged and attentive.

For instance, insert quick polls or interactive quizzes within presentations to maintain audience focus and involvement.

6. **Use technology**: Use tools like online polls, virtual whiteboards, or chat rooms to encourage participation and interaction.

For instance, create a chat room for real-time discussions during virtual events to promote active participation

7. **Be responsive**: Respond to questions and comments in a timely and respectful manner. This encourages people to keep engaging and interacting.

8. **Provide feedback**: Give positive feedback and constructive criticism to encourage people to keep participating and improve their skills.

9. **Provide value:** To keep members engaged, it's important to offer them value. This could be in the form of exclusive

content, discounts or anything else that's relevant to their interests and needs.

For instance, offer exclusive content such as expert interviews or early access to resources as a reward for active participation.

---

10. **Encourage participation:** Make it easy for members to participate in discussions by providing clear prompts, asking for feedback, and creating opportunities for them to share their own experiences.

11. **Use gamification**: Gamification can be a fun way to encourage engagement in your online community. This could involve offering rewards or badges for completing certain actions, or creating a leaderboard to show who is the most active member.

For instance, implement a 'Member of the Month' recognition program with badges and rewards for active engagement.

---

12. **Host events:** Virtual events such as webinars, Q&A sessions, or live chats can be a great way to foster engagement and interaction. They allow members to connect with each other and with your brand in a more personal way.

13. **Leverage social media:** Use social media to promote your online community and encourage members to share their experiences. You could also use social media to

share content from the community, such as user-generated content or highlights from events.

For instance, create a hashtag for community members to share their experiences to help foster a sense of community across platforms

---

By using these strategies, you can create a thriving online community that stimulates engagement and interaction among its members, leading to increased loyalty and advocacy for your brand.

How to Handle Negative Comments and Feedback

Receiving negative comments and feedback can be difficult, but it is important to handle them in a professional and constructive manner. So, here are some steps you can take:

1. **Don't take it personally:** Remember that negative comments are not necessarily a reflection of you as a person, but rather a response to a specific action or situation.

2. **Listen and try to understand:** Take the time to really listen to the feedback and try to understand the other person's perspective. Ask questions if necessary to clarify their points.

3. **Stay calm and professional:** Responding with anger or defensiveness will only make the situation worse. Stay calm and respond in a professional manner.

4. **Thank the person for their feedback**: Even if you don't agree with their criticism, thank the person for taking the time to share their thoughts with you.

5. **Address the issue**: If there is a specific issue that needs to be addressed, take steps to do so. Explain what you are doing to address the issue and how you plan to prevent it from happening again in the future.

6. **Use the feedback to improve:** Negative feedback can be a valuable learning experience. Use it to identify areas where you can improve and make changes as necessary.

Remember, handling negative feedback in a constructive and professional manner can honestly help to improve your reputation and build stronger relationships with your customers or clients.

Chapter 8

LEVERAGING SOCIAL MEDIA FOR IDEAL LEADERSHIP

Leveraging social media for ideal leadership involves using various social media platforms to establish yourself or your brand as an authority in your industry or field. It's a way of sharing your ideas, insights, and expertise with your target audience to build trust, credibility, and influence.

Below are some ways you can leverage social media for ideal leadership:

1. **Share your knowledge:** Share your insights, opinions, and experiences on relevant topics in your industry or field through blog posts, videos, and social media updates. Provide value to your audience by offering tips, advice, and solutions to their problems.

2. **Engage with your audience:** Respond to comments, answer questions, and participate in relevant conversations with your followers. This will help you build a relationship with your audience and establish yourself as an approachable and helpful ideal leader.

3. **Participate in industry conversations:** Join industry-specific groups, participate in Twitter chats, and attend relevant conferences to stay up-to-date on industry trends and engage with other ideal leaders in your field.

4. **Use visuals:** Use high-quality images, infographics, and videos to showcase your ideas and make them more engaging and shareable.

5. **Be consistent:** Consistently share valuable content and engage with your audience to stay top-of-mind and establish yourself as a trusted ideal leader in your industry or field.

By leveraging social media for ideal leadership, you can establish yourself or your brand as an authority in your industry or field, build a loyal following, and increase your influence and reach.

Establishing yourself as an Ideal Leader in your Industry

Establishing yourself as an ideal leader in your industry means that you are recognized as an expert and a respected authority in your field. It means that you are seen as someone who has a deep understanding of the industry and its challenges, and you are able to provide unique insights, innovative ideas, and solutions to complex problems.

Being an outstanding leader requires more than just having expertise and knowledge. It also involves sharing your knowledge and insights with others through various channels, such as writing articles, giving speeches, participating in industry events, or creating content on social media.

- ➤ Stay informed about industry trends, technologies, and best practices.

- ➤ Attend relevant workshops, webinars, and conferences to enhance your knowledge.

- ➤ Attend industry events, join professional organizations, and engage with peers. It will help you build relationships, exchange ideas, and gain exposure.

- ➤ Specialize in a niche within your industry and known as an expert by consistently producing high-quality work and staying up-to-date with the latest developments.

- ➤ Establish a strong online presence through social media, a professional website, and industry forums. Share your insights, achievements, and contribute to discussions.

- ➤ Create and share valuable content, such as blog posts, articles, and other relevant content.

- ➤ Mentor others in your industry and collaborate on projects. It will help contribute to your industry's growth and also enhances your leadership reputation.

- ➤ Hone your communication skills by clearly communicating your ideas, whether in presentations, written content, or interpersonal interactions.

➢ Demonstrate the values and work ethic you expect from others. Lead by example to inspire trust and respect among your peers and team.

➢ Embrace change and adapt to new circumstances. A leader who can navigate challenges and guide others through transitions is highly qualified and regarded.

➢ Develop strong problem-solving skills as leaders who can find innovative solutions to challenges are often seen as indispensable.

➢ Empathy fosters positive relationships and demonstrates effective leadership. So, understand the needs and concerns of your team and industry peers.

➢ Develop a strategic mindset. Leaders who can envision the future and guide their teams toward long-term goals and objectives are well-respected.

➢ Showcase your achievements and successful projects. A track record of success will help enhances your credibility as a leader.

➢ Be open to feedback and continually seek opportunities for improvement.

Establishing yourself as an ideal leader in your industry involves strategic actions, consistent efforts and when you establish yourself as an ideal leader, you become a go-to source for information or advice in your industry.

When people trust your opinions, insights and turn to you for guidance, it can help you build a strong reputation, attract new clients or customers and also help you advance your career.

Developing a Personal Brand on Social Media

Developing a personal brand on social media involves crafting a unique and consistent identity that reflects your values, expertise, and personality. It requires creating a cohesive online presence across platforms, engaging with your audience, and strategically sharing content to build an authentic and memorable digital image.

Developing a personal brand on social media can be an effective way to establish yourself as an idea leader in your industry and build your professional reputation.

Developing a strong personal brand on social media takes dedication and strategy, but the rewards can be worth it. Here are some detailed tips for developing a strong personal brand on social media:

1. Define your niche and target audience: Identify your area of expertise and the people you want to reach with your content.
> ➢ What are you passionate about?
> ➢ What expertise or unique perspective can you offer?
> ➢ Who are you trying to reach?
> ➢ What platform fits best?

Different platforms appeal to different audiences and content styles. So choose the platforms where your target audience is most active.

2. Create a consistent brand image: Your profile picture, cover photo, bio, and tone of voice should be consistent across all social media platforms to help build brand recognition.

> ➢ Create a concise and memorable bio that captures your essence.
> ➢ Use consistent visuals and tone across all platforms.

3. Share valuable and high-quality content: Share your insights, expertise, and valuable information related to your niche. This will enable you to earn yourself a title as a credible source of information.

> ➢ Focus on providing value and entertainment for your audience.
> ➢ Use a mix of formats such as text, images, videos, and live streams.
> ➢ Be informative, engaging, and visually appealing.
> ➢ Most importantly, stay consistent with your posting schedule.

4. Engage with your audience: Respond to comments, participate in conversations, and engage with your followers to build relationships and establish trust.

> ➢ Respond to comments and messages promptly.
> ➢ Ask questions and spark conversations.
> ➢ Participate in relevant hashtags and discussions.
> ➢ Run contests and giveaways to boost engagement.

5. Collaborate and network: Connect with other influencers and brands in your niche.

> ➤ Do guest posts, interviews, or joint projects.
> ➤ Seek opportunities to speak at events or to be featured in an online publication.

6. Be authentic: Be true to yourself and your values. Don't try to be someone you're not, and always be transparent about your successes and failures.

7. Regularly monitor your online presence and respond to any negative comments or feedback in a professional and respectful manner.

Developing a strong personal brand on social media is a rewarding and empowering experience. By following the tips above and staying dedicated, you can build a loyal following, expand your reach, and achieve your personal or professional goals. These are just a starting point, be free to delve deeper into any of the mentioned tips.

Creating and Sharing Ideal Leadership Content

In today's digital age, effective leadership goes beyond just making decisions and managing teams. It requires inspiring, influencing, and connecting with your audience both within and outside your organization. And one of the most powerful and reliable ways to achieve this is through creating and sharing ideal leadership content.

Ideal leadership content are content that goes beyond the usual motivational quotes and generic advice. This content are thoughtful, insightful, and actionable while also offering valuable perspectives and practical strategies that your audience can implement in their lives.

Ideal content should:

1. **Be based on your unique expertise and experience.**
   - ➢ What makes you a different kind of leader?
   - ➢ What lessons have you learned along the way?

2. **Address current challenges and trends.**
   - ➢ What are the pressing issues facing leaders today?
   - ➢ How can your content offer solutions or ignite meaningful conversations?

3. **Provide actionable takeaways.**
   - ➢ Don't just inspire. Equip your audience with detailed and concrete steps they can take to enhance and improve their leadership skills.

4. **Be engaging and informative.**
   - ➢ Use storytelling, data, humor, or visuals to keep your audience focused and hooked up so they can keep coming back for more.

Creating and sharing ideal leadership content is an effective way to establish yourself as an expert in your industry and build a strong personal brand.

Types of Ideal Leadership Content

Here are some types of ideal leadership content you can create:

1. **Blog posts.**
   - Share your thoughts on relevant topics.
   - Offer practical tips and solutions.
   - Analyze case studies.

2. **Articles.**
   - Contribute to industry publications and online platforms to reach a broader audience.

3. **Videos.**
   - Host Q&A sessions.
   - Deliver mini-lessons.
   - Share behind-the-scenes.

4. **Podcasts**.
   - Interview other leaders.
   - Discuss current trends and topics.
   - Provide in-depth insights.

5. **Social media posts.**
   - Share valuable content.
   - Engage in conversations and connect with your audience on a personal level.

Ideal leadership content should be focused on providing value to your audience and establishing your expertise in your industry.

Tips for Creating Ideal Leadership Content

Creating impactful leadership content isn't about broadcasting pronouncements. It requires intentionality, clarity, and a strategic approach to reach the hearts and minds of your audience.

> **Identify your unique perspective:** To create ideal leadership content, you need to have a unique perspective on your industry. Identify what sets you apart from others in your field and use that as the basis for your content.

> **Know your target audience:** Who are you trying to reach with your content? Are they aspiring entrepreneurs, established executives, or community leaders facing new challenges? Determine your target audience and create content that communicates directly to their needs and interests.

> **Choose the right format: Ideal** leadership content can take many different forms, such as blog posts, videos, podcasts and more. Decide on the format that suits your goals and target audience.

> **Provide value:** Your content should provide valuable insights, ideas, and solutions related to your industry. Avoid self-promotion and focus on providing value to your audience.

> **Share your content:** Share your content on social media, industry forums, and other relevant platforms to reach a wider audience.

➢ **Repurpose your content:** Repurpose your content into different formats to reach a wider audience. For instance, you can turn a blog post into a video or a podcast.

➢ **Monitor your results:** Monitor the performance of your content and adjust your strategy as needed. Track metrics such as views, engagement, and conversions to measure the impact of your ideal leadership content.

Tips for Sharing Ideal Leadership Content Effectively

1. **Firstly, identify the right platforms** and focus on the platforms they use most often.

2. **Secondly, optimize your content for each platform.** Each platform has its own audience and language. Tailor your content and tone to fit in. Facebook might call for engaging narratives, while LinkedIn caters to concise and professional insights.

3. **Promote your content strategically** by utilizing social media tools, collaborate with other influencers, and engage in relevant online communities.

4. **Analyze your content's performance** to see what's working and what's not. Adapt your strategy based on your findings.

5. **Focus on stories and examples** as people tends to connect with stories more than dry facts and figures. Use

real-life examples to illustrate your points and make your content more relatable.

6. **Be vulnerable and authentic.** Don't be afraid to share your own challenges and failures. This will make you appear more relatable to your audience.

7. **Be clear and concise.** Get to the point quickly and avoid using jargon or overly technical language.

8. **Use high-quality images,** videos, and infographics to break up your text and make your content more engaging.

By following these tips and staying committed to creating valuable content, you can become a thoughtful leader in your field and inspire others to reach their full potential.

Chapter 9

MEASURING SOCIAL MEDIA SUCCESS

Measuring social media success is the process of evaluating the effectiveness of your social media strategies and tactics in achieving your business goals. The exact metrics you use to measure success will depend on your specific goals and objectives. Here are some commonly used metrics for measuring social media success:

1. **Engagement metrics:** These metrics measure how much your audience is interacting with your content. This includes likes, comments, shares, and retweets.

2. **Followers growth:** This metric measures how many people are following your social media accounts over time.

3. **Traffic and conversion metrics:** These metrics measure how much traffic your social media channels are driving to your website and how many of those visitors are converting into customers.

4. **Reach and impressions:** Reach measures how many people are seeing your content, while impressions measure how many times your content is being viewed.

5. **Brand sentiment:** This metric measures how positively or negatively people are talking about your brand on social media.

6. **Return on investment (ROI):** This metric measures the financial return on your social media investment.

By tracking and analyzing these metrics, you can gain insights into the effectiveness of your social media efforts and adjust your strategies accordingly.

Key Performance Indicators for Social Media Success

There are specific metrics that you use to measure the success of your social media marketing efforts. Here are some common KPIs to consider:

1. **Engagement rate:** This KPI measures how often your audience interacts with your content. It is calculated by dividing the total number of engagements by the total number of impressions and expressing the result as a percentage.

2. **Follower growth rate:** This KPI measures the rate at which your social media followers are increasing over time.

3. **Click-through rate (CTR):** This KPI measures the number of clicks your social media posts generate compared to the total number of impressions.

4. **Conversion rate:** This KPI measures the percentage of social media users who take a desired action on your website after clicking on a social media post.

5. **Customer acquisition cost (CAC):** This KPI measures the cost of acquiring new customers through social media marketing.

6. **Return on investment (ROI):** This KPI measures the financial return on your social media investment, comparing the revenue generated to the costs incurred.

It's important to choose KPIs that align with your overall business goals and objectives. By tracking and analyzing these metrics, you can gain insights into the effectiveness of your social media marketing efforts and make data-driven decisions to improve your performance.

Let's illustrate the significance of these KPIs using an example: For instance, you own a fashion brand and want more people to know about it and buy your awesome clothes. One important thing to check is your engagement rate which is like keeping an eye on how much people like and comment on your posts about new clothes or cool discounts.

Let's say you make your posts look super cool, and suddenly more people start liking and commenting, which increased your engagement rate from 5% to 10%. That means your posts are grabbing people's attention and making them excited about your design or post.

Now, think about your follower growth rate. If more people start following your brand on social media (let's say 15% more), that's like building a bigger fan club, which is great because you want more people to know about your fashion brand, and it might even bring more customers to your real shop.

Next up is the click-through rate (CTR). This is like checking if your posts are super interesting that people want to see more on your website. Let's say for instance, your CTR goes up from 2% to 5% which proves that more people are clicking on your posts and checking out your online store. And when your CTR increases it's likely to lead to more people buying your clothes.

Now, the conversion rate is a big deal. It's like seeing if people actually bought something after visiting your website. So, let's say you try a cool discount campaign on social media, and suddenly more people buys stuff which increased your conversion rate from 2% to 4%. This means your strategy worked, and people liked the discounts enough to make a purchase.

And guess what? Your Customer Acquisition Cost (CAC) drops by 20%, which signifies that you found a smarter way to tell people about your brand, and it costs less. So, you're getting more customers without spending too much money.

Finally, you calculate the Return on Investment (ROI). This is a way of measuring how much money you earned from social media than you spent on it.

So, in the end, these numbers tell a story. They show that your social media plan is making more people excited about your brand, bringing in new customers, and even boosting your sales.

Tools for Tracking and Analyzing Social Media Metrics

Tracking and analyzing social media metrics is essential for measuring the success of a social media campaign and making data-driven decisions to improve engagement and reach. Below are some tools and techniques for tracking and analyzing social media metrics:

1. **Social media analytics tools**: There are many social media analytics tools available that can help you track metrics such as reach, engagement, and conversions. Some popular options include Hootsuite, Sprout Social, Buffer, and Google Analytics.

2. **Social media monitoring tools**: Social media monitoring tools help you track mentions and conversations related to your brand or industry. This can provide valuable insights into customer sentiment and help you identify potential issues early on.

3. **Key performance indicators (KPIs):** This help determines which KPIs are most relevant to your business goals, such as follower growth, engagement rate, click-through rate, or conversion rate. This will allow you to focus on the metrics that matter broadly to your business.

4. **Competitive analysis:** Analyzing your competitors' social media metrics can help you benchmark your performance and identify areas where you need to improve. You can use tools like Socialbakers and Brandwatch to track your competitors' social media activity.

5. **A/B testing**: Experiment with different social media tactics and analyze the results to see what works best for your audience. For example, you can test different types of content, posting times, and hashtags to see which ones generate the most engagement.

6. **Regular reporting**: Set up a regular reporting schedule to track your progress over time and identify trends. This will help you make data-driven decisions and adjust your strategy as needed.

Tracking and analyzing social media metrics requires a combination of tools, techniques, and regular reporting. By focusing on the metrics that matter most to your business goals, you can improve your social media strategy and achieve better results.

Tools for Tracking and Analyzing Social Media Metrics

1. **Hootsuite.**
   ○ **Official Website:** https://www.hootsuite.com/

Use: Social media analytics tool for tracking metrics such as reach, engagement, and conversions. It allows you to schedule posts, manage multiple social media platforms, and gain insights into audience behavior.

2. **Sprout Social.**
   ○ **Official Website:** https://sproutsocial.com/

Use: Social media management and analytics tool. It helps track follower growth, engagement rate, and conversion rate. Additionally, Sprout Social provides collaboration features for social media teams.

3. **Buffer.**
   ○ **Official Website:** https://buffer.com/

Use: Social media analytics tool which focuses on scheduling posts. Buffer allows A/B testing by experimenting with different posting times, content types, and analyzing the results for optimal engagement.

4. **Google Analytics**
   ○ **Official Website:** https://analytics.google.com/

Use: Google Analytics offers website analytics. It helps in understanding user behavior, traffic sources, and the impact of social media on website conversions.

5. **Brandwatch**
   ○ **Official Website:** https://www.brandwatch.com/

Use: Social media monitoring tool for tracking brand mentions and conversations. It aids in understanding customer sentiment, identifying trends, and addressing potential issues proactively.

6. **Socialbakers**
   ○ **Official Website:** https://www.socialbakers.com/

Use: Socialbakers is a competitive analysis tool that allows you to compare your social media metrics with competitors. It provides insights into industry trends and helps refine your social media strategy based on competitive performance.

These mentioned tools collectively support a robust social media strategy by offering analytics, monitoring, collaboration, and performance comparison capabilities. Choose the ones that align best with your business goals and objectives.

Using Insights to Inform Strategy and Improve Results

Businesses have access to a vast amount of information about their customers, markets, and operations in today's data-driven world. But just collecting data is not enough. The true power lies in transforming that data into actionable insights that can inform your strategy and drive better results.

Insights are meaningful patterns, trends, and connections that reveal deeper understanding about your business. They answer the "why" and "how" behind the numbers, providing you with a clear picture of what's working and what's not.

How Insights Inform Strategy

1. It helps understand customer needs and preferences to develop products and services they truly value.

2. It helps target the right audience with the right message at the right time and also optimize your campaigns for maximum impact.

3. It helps identify areas for improvement in efficiency, reduce costs, and streamline processes.

4. It helps build a strong and engaged workforce by understanding employee needs and motivations.

By understanding your customers better, you can deliver products and services that meet their needs and exceed their expectations.

Examples of Using Insights to Improve Results:

➤ A clothing retailer analyzes customer purchase data to discover that a particular color of shirt is consistently selling out. They use this insight to increase production of that color which will lead to higher sales and reduced inventory costs.

➤ A streaming service tracks user viewing habits to identify popular genres and binge-watching patterns. They use this insight to recommend similar content to users to increase engagement and retention.

The Benefits of Using Insights:

➢ Data-driven decisions are more likely to be successful than gut-based decisions.

➢ Insights can help you identify and eliminate waste in your operations.

➢ Businesses that effectively use insights achieve a significant edge over their competitors.

Getting Started with Insights

Using insights to inform strategy and improve results is a crucial aspect of any business or marketing plan. Here are some steps you can take to use insights to improve your strategy and achieve better results:

1. **Set clear objectives:** Determine your business goals and the key performance indicators (KPIs) that will help you measure progress. This will help you focus on the metrics that matter most to your business and identify areas where you need to improve.

2. **Collect and analyze data:** Use tools and techniques, such as social media analytics, website analytics, customer feedback, and market research, to collect and analyze data related to your business and industry. This will help you understand your audience's behavior, preferences, and needs, as well as your competitors' strengths and weaknesses.

3. **Identify trends and patterns:** Look for patterns and trends in your data to identify areas where you can improve. For example, if you notice that your website has a high bounce rate, you may need to improve your website design or content to make it more engaging.

4. **Make data-driven decisions:** Use your insights to inform your business and marketing strategy. For example, if you notice that your audience is more engaged with video content, you may want to invest more in creating video content for your social media channels.

5. **Test and iterate:** Test different strategies and tactics to see what works best for your business. For example, you may want to test different ad copy or landing page designs to see which ones generate the most conversions. Use your insights to iterate and improve your approach over time.

6. **Monitor and report:** Monitor your progress over time and report on your results regularly. This will help you track your progress towards your goals and make adjustments as needed.

Using insights to inform strategy and improve results requires a continuous cycle of data collection, analysis, decision-making, and testing. By taking a data-driven approach, you can make informed decisions that will help you achieve your business goals and improve your results.

Chapter 10

MANAGING SOCIAL MEDIA RISK

Managing social media risk is the process of identifying, assessing, and mitigating the potential negative consequences that can arise from the use of social media. Social media risk can take various forms, including reputational damage, legal liability, data breaches, and cyber-attacks.

Effective management of social media risk requires organizations to develop comprehensive social media policies and guidelines, provide employee training, monitor social media activity, and implement appropriate security measures. It also involves having a plan in place to respond to negative incidents that may occur on social media, such as a crisis communication plan. By managing social media risk, organizations can reduce the likelihood of negative consequences and protect their brand reputation, while also leveraging social media's benefits to reach and engage with their target audience. Here are some tips to help you manage social media risk:

1. **Develop a social media policy:** A social media policy outlines guidelines for employees to follow when using social media. It should include guidelines for acceptable content, confidentiality, and privacy.

2. **Monitor social media:** Regularly monitoring social media can help you stay aware of what's being said about your brand, products, or services. This will allow you to respond quickly to any negative comments or complaints.

3. **Train employees:** Make sure that employees understand the social media policy and are trained in how to use social media safely and responsibly.

4. **Use strong passwords:** Ensure that all social media accounts have strong passwords, and that they are changed regularly.

5. **Limit access:** Only give access to social media accounts to employees who need it for their job, and ensure that they understand the risks involved.

6. **Have a crisis plan:** In case of a social media crisis, have a plan in place to address the situation quickly and effectively.

7. **Stay up-to-date:** Keep up-to-date with the latest social media trends and security issues, and adjust your policies and procedures as necessary.

Understanding and Mitigating Social Media Risks

Social media can present a variety of risks to businesses and individuals, such as reputation damage, cyberbullying, identity theft, data breaches, and more. Below are some of the most common social media risks and how to mitigating them:

1. **Data/Privacy Breach:** Unauthorized access and acquisition of sensitive information. During a data breach, cybercriminals gain access to databases, networks, or systems to obtain personal, financial, or other valuable data.

Mitigation;

- ➢ Implement strong security measures.
- ➢ Encryption sensitive information to protect it even if unauthorized access occurs.
- ➢ Utilize strict access controls and permissions to limit who can access sensitive data.
- ➢ Conduct regular security audits to identify vulnerabilities in systems and networks.
- ➢ Segregate networks to compartmentalize data to help limit the impact of a breach to a specific segment.
- ➢ Utilize real-time monitoring and intrusion detection systems to identify unusual activities.
- ➢ Establish a dedicated incident response team to handle and investigate security incidents.
- ➢ Keep all software, including security software and applications updated with the latest patches.
- ➢ Regularly backup critical data to ensure recovery in case of a breach or data loss.

➢ Consider obtaining cyber insurance to help mitigate financial losses associated with a data breach.

2.   Reputation Damage: This refers to the harm or negative impact on an individual, organization and public perception. Reputation damage often lead to loss of trust, customer loyalty, and credibility, which affects long-term success and relationships.

Mitigation:
➢ Communicate transparently and proactively address issues as they arise.
➢ Develop a comprehensive crisis management plan to effectively handle reputation-threatening situations.
➢ Use social listening tools to track and monitor online conversations and sentiment about the brand.
➢ Prioritize customer satisfaction and promptly address customer concerns or complaints.
➢ Train employees on representing the brand positively and avoiding behaviors that could harm reputation.
➢ Implement good strategies to manage and enhance the brand's online presence.
➢ Maintain consistency in brand messaging, values, and image across all communication channels.
➢ Actively engage with stakeholders, including employees, customers, and the community.
➢ Ensure strict adherence to legal and ethical standards in business practices.
➢ Build and maintain positive relationships with the media.
➢ Regularly assess and improve services, products, and operations based on feedback.

3. **Cybersecurity Threats (Phishing, malware and account hijacking):** Phishing is a deceptive attempt to obtain sensitive information, malware refers to malicious software designed to harm systems, while account hijacking involves unauthorized access to and control over user accounts.

Mitigation:

> Use Multi-Factor Authentication (MFA)
> Implement email security protocols. (Use SPF, DKIM, and DMARC to combat phishing)
> Install antivirus software and update systems regularly.
> Conduct audits to identify and address vulnerabilities.
> Enforce strong password policies for users.
> Educate users about phishing risks and safe online practices.
> Have a predefined plan to respond effectively to security incidents.
> Implement firewalls, secure Wi-Fi, and VPNs.
> Keep users informed about upcoming threats.

4. **Fake Accounts and Impersonation:** Fake accounts and impersonation are fraudulent profiles or online personas, often mimicking legitimate individuals or organizations, with the intent to deceive and manipulate others.

Mitigation

> Establish and promote clear reporting mechanisms for users to report suspected fake accounts or impersonation.
> Apply account verification processes, such as badges for legitimate profiles to help users identify authentic accounts.

- ➤ Educate users on how to recognize fake accounts.
- ➤ Deploy automated detection systems to identify and flag suspicious account activities, patterns, or anomalies.
- ➤ Apply secure authentication methods, like two-factor authentication to enhance the security of user accounts.
- ➤ Regularly conduct audits to identify and remove fake account to ensure a clean and trustworthy online environment.
- ➤ Take legal action against individuals or entities engaged in malicious impersonation, when necessary.
- ➤ Establish a quick response system to investigate and take appropriate action upon receiving reports of fake accounts or impersonation.
- ➤ Collaborate with social media platforms and online communities to address and remove fake accounts.
- ➤ Empower users with strong privacy settings to control the visibility of their personal information to help reduce the potential for misuse.
- ➤ Continuously monitor online spaces for signs of impersonation or the creation of fake accounts.

5. Intellectual Property Issues: This involves the unauthorized use, infringement, or misappropriation of creative works, inventions, trademarks, or trade secrets protected by intellectual property laws.

Mitigation:
- ➤ Register relevant intellectual property (IP) with appropriate authorities and maintain comprehensive documentation to establish ownership.

➢ Seek legal counsel specializing in intellectual property law to provide guidance, handle registrations, and to also address infringement issues.

➢ Train employees on the importance of respecting intellectual property rights and how to handle proprietary information properly.

➢ Implement confidentiality agreements (non-disclosure agreements) with employees, contractors, and partners to protect sensitive informations.

➢ Regularly conduct audits of intellectual property holdings and usage to identify and address potential infringements.

➢ Establish clear internal policies and guidelines regarding the use, protection, and respect of intellectual property.

➢ Use monitoring tools to identify unauthorized use or infringement, and take legal action to enforce intellectual property rights.

➢ Enter into licensing agreements when appropriate and outline terms for the authorized use of intellectual property by others.

➢ Raise public awareness about intellectual property rights to deter infringement.

➢ Apply strong cybersecurity measures to secure digital assets and prevent unauthorized access or theft of intellectual property.

➢ Consider international protections, such as filing for trademarks in relevant jurisdictions to safeguard intellectual property globally.

➢ Explore alternative dispute resolution methods, such as mediation or arbitration, to resolve intellectual property disputes efficiently.

6. Spread of misinformation: This is to the dissemination of false or misleading information, often through various channels, which can lead to misunderstandings and potential harm.

Mitigation:
- ➢ Promote fact-checking organizations that verify information and debunk false claims to counter the spread of misinformation.
- ➢ Encourage media outlets and platforms to be transparent in reporting, disclosing sources and providing context to information.
- ➢ Promote and share content from trusted and reputable sources, helping to elevate accurate information in the public domain.
- ➢ Step up mechanisms for users to report and flag content they believe to be misinformation.
- ➢ Collaborate with social media platforms to identify and limit the spread of misinformation.
- ➢ Communicate clearly and consistently, especially during crises, to provide accurate information and address potential misinformation promptly.
- ➢ Use public service announcements to disseminate accurate information and correct misconceptions on various topics.
- ➢ Platforms should consider adjusting algorithms to prioritize and amplify content from reputable sources over misinformation.
- ➢ Create a crisis communication plans to address the spread of misinformation during emergencies to ensure a coordinated and accurate response.
- ➢ Engage with communities to build trust and foster open dialogues.

Developing a Social Media Policy for Your Organization

A Social Media Policy is a set of rules and guidelines established by an organization to govern the use of social media platforms by its employees, representatives, or members. Creating a social media policy for your organization is an important step to ensure that employees understand how to use social media in a responsible and professional manner.

Here's a step-by-step guide on how to create social media;

1. **Define Objectives and Scope:**
   - Clearly outline the goals and objectives of the Social Media Policy.
   - Specify the scope, including which individuals it applies to (employees, volunteers, etc.).

2. **Legal and Regulatory Review:**
   - Consult with legal professionals to understand and comply with relevant laws and regulations regarding to social media use in your industry and location.

3. **Identify Key Stakeholders:**
   - Involve key stakeholders, including legal, HR, communications, and IT professionals.

4. **Conduct a Risk Assessment:**
   - Identify common and potential risks associated with social media use for your organization.
   - Consider reputational, legal, and security risks.

5. **Benchmark Best Practices:**
   - Research and benchmark social media policies from similar organizations or industry leaders.
   - Include best practices and relevant guidelines.

6. **Establish Clear Guidelines:**
   - Define acceptable and unacceptable behavior on social media platforms.
   - Include guidelines on professionalism, respect, and ethical conduct.

7. **Address Confidentiality and Privacy:**
   - Clearly articulate rules regarding the sharing of confidential information and respecting privacy.
   - Provide guidance on protecting organizational and personal data.

8. **Define Employee Representation:**
   - Specify how employees should represent the organization on social media.
   - Encourage transparency about personal views not reflecting organizational positions.

9. **Incorporate Cybersecurity Measures:**
   - Include guidelines on securing professional and personal social media accounts.
   - Encourage the use of strong passwords and two-factor authentication.

10. **Create a Reporting Mechanism:** Establish a clear and confidential reporting mechanism in case of policy violations

11. Educational Initiatives:
> - Develop training programs or materials to educate employees about the Social Media Policy.
> - Include information on digital literacy, cybersecurity, and responsible social media use.

12. Review and Approval:
> - Circulate the draft policy among key stakeholders for review and feedback.
> - Seek finalizing approval from leadership and legal teams.

13. Communication and Rollout:
> - Communicate the new Social Media Policy to all relevant individuals.
> - Conduct training sessions to ensure understanding.

14. Regular Review and Updates:
> - Periodically review and update the policy to reflect changes in technology, laws and organizational needs.
> - Communicate updates to all stakeholders.

15. Employee Acknowledgment:
> - Require employees to acknowledge understanding and agreement with the Social Media Policy.

16. Enforcement and Consequences:
> - Outline consequences for policy violations.

17. Monitor and Adapt:
> - Monitor social media activities regularly for compliance.

Social Media Policy Example

Social Media Policy for [Organization Name]

Date: [Effective Date]

Purpose

The purpose of this social media policy is to provide guidelines for [Organization Name]'s employees, contractors, and representatives when engaging in social media activities on behalf of the organization.

Acceptable Use

➢ All social media activities representing [Organization Name] must align with the organization's values, mission, and policies.

➢ Respect all applicable laws, including privacy laws and copyright regulations.

Professional Conduct

➢ Be careful of the organization's image and reputation. Exercise professionalism and good judgment in all online interactions.

➢ Views expressed are personal and do not necessarily represent [Organization Name].

Confidentiality

➤ Do not disclose confidential information or proprietary company data or information. Obtain necessary approvals before sharing any non-public information.

➤ Respect the privacy of colleagues, partners and clients.

Brand Representation

➤ Adhere to the organization's brand guidelines when creating and sharing content. Use approved logos and consistently use branding elements.

➤ Report any unauthorized use or misrepresentation of the organization's brand.

Personal Responsibility

➤ Clearly differentiate between personal and organizational social media accounts.

➤ Express personal opinions carefully. [Emphasize they are individual views]

➤ Report any online harassment promptly and avoid engaging in online disputes or arguments.

Content Creation

➤ Obtain necessary permissions when using third-party content. Give appropriate credit when using or referencing external materials.

- ➢ Refrain from posting misleading information or engaging in activities that could harm the reputation of the organization.

Security Measures

- ➢ Use strong and unique passwords for all social media accounts associated with [Organization Name]. Most importantly, update passwords regularly.

- ➢ Immediately report any suspicious activity, phishing attempts, or potential security breaches.

Reporting Violations

- ➢ Promptly report any violations of this policy to the designated supervisor or the IT/security department.

- ➢ [Encourage a culture of accountability and ethical behavior among colleagues]

Training and Awareness

- ➢ Participate in social media training sessions provided by the organization.

- ➢ Stay informed about updates on social media policies and best practices.

Consequences of Violations

Violations of this social media policy may result in disciplinary action, up to and including termination of employment or contractual relationship.

Review and Updates

This policy will be periodically reviewed and updated to reflect changes made in social media trends, technologies, or organizational requirements.

By adhering to this social media policy, we ensure a positive online presence that reflects the values and professionalism of [Organization Name].

Acknowledgement

I have read and understood [Organization Name]'s Social Media Policy. I agree to comply with its guidelines and understand the consequences of violating this policy.

Employee/Representative Name: [Printed Name]
Signature: _____
Date: [Effective Date]

Customize your social media policy based on your organization's specific needs, industry regulations, and legal considerations. Consult with relevant professionals to ensure legal compliance and effectiveness.

Preparing for Social Media Crisis

Social media can be a powerful tool for businesses, but it also has its own set of risks. One of the biggest dangers is the potential for a social media crisis. A single misstep, negative press, or just a little misunderstanding can quickly turn into a PR nightmare. That's why it's important to be prepared for social media crises before they strike. And by having a plan in place, you can minimize the damage and protect your brand's reputation. Here are effective ways to prepare for social media crises;

1. **Establish a Crisis Management Team.**
   - ➢ Appoint a team responsible for handling social media crisis. Include representatives from public relations, legal, social media management, and relevant departments.

2. **Develop a Crisis Response Plan.**
   - ➢ Create detailed procedures for identifying, assessing, and responding to potential crisis. *Clearly define roles and responsibilities within the crisis management team.*

3. **Monitor Social Media Channels.**
   - ➢ Apply strong monitoring tools to track mentions, comments, and discussions related to your brand. Early detection is important for a swift response.

4. **Define Trigger Points**
   - ➢ Set up specific trigger points that indicate when a situation escalates to crisis level. These could include the volume of negative mentions, potential legal implications, or significant social media engagement.

5. **Pre-draft Crisis Messages.**
   - ➢ Prepare pre-drafted crisis messages for various scenarios. Tailor these messages to address potential issues to ensure a timely and consistent response.

6. Identify Spokespersons.

> Appoint trained spokespeople who will represent the organization during a crisis. Ensure they are well-versed in the organization's messaging and also available for immediate response.

7. Coordinate with Legal.

> Work closely with legal teams to understand potential legal implications of different crises. Ensure that responses adhere to legal requirements and protect the organization's interests.

8. Establish Communication Protocols.

> Define internal and external communication protocols. Choose and determine how information will be disseminated within the organization and to the public.

9. Train Employees.

> Provide regular training to employees on crisis communication procedures and ensure that employees understand their roles and responsibilities in the event of a social media crisis.

10. Regularly Update Contact Information.

> Keep an up-to-date list of contacts for the crisis management team, legal representatives, key executives, and relevant stakeholders to ensure quick and efficient communication during a crisis.

11. Test Crisis Response Plans.

➢ Conduct exercises to test the effectiveness of your crisis response plans and evaluate the team's ability to execute the plan and identify areas for improvement.

12. **Learn from Past Incidents.**
➢ Conduct thorough post-crisis reviews to analyze the organization's response. Then, also identify lessons learned and update crisis response plans accordingly.

13. **Establish Post-Crisis Communication.**
➢ Develop a strategy for rebuilding the organization's image after a crisis. Communicate transparently, take corrective actions, and exhibit a commitment to improvement.

14. **Leverage Social Listening.**
➢ Utilize social listening tools to understand public sentiment and track ongoing conversations post-crisis. Adjust strategies based on the feedback received.

By proactively preparing for social media crises, your organization can respond effectively, minimize damage, and protect its reputation in the digital landscape. Most importantly, regularly review and update crisis management plans to stay resilient in the face of evolving challenges.

Social Media Crisis Response Plan

Objective

This document outlines the procedures for identifying, assessing, and responding to potential crises on social media platforms. The aim is to ensure a swift, coordinated, and effective response to protect the reputation and interests of [Organization Name].

Crisis Management Team

- Crisis Manager: [Name]
- Spokesperson: [Name]
- Legal Representative: [Name]
- Social Media Manager: [Name]
- Communications Specialist: [Name]
- IT/Security Representative: [Name]
- [Other Relevant Roles]

Identification of Social Media Crises

1. **Monitoring;**
   - Use social media monitoring tools to track brand mentions, comments, and discussions.
   - Develop regular monitoring schedules to detect potential issues early.

2. **Trigger Points;**
   - Define specific trigger points that indicate when a situation escalates to a crisis level.
   - Examples: Volume of negative mentions, potential legal implications, significant social media engagement.

Assessment of Crisis Severity

1. **Categorization**;
   - Classify crises into categories based on severity and potential impact on the organization.
   - Categories: Low, Moderate, High, Critical.

2. **Impact Analysis:**
   - Assess the potential impact of each crisis category on the organization's reputation, stakeholders, and operations.

Response Procedures

1. **Activation of Crisis Management Team;**
   - Crisis Manager to assess severity and activate the crisis management team as needed.
   - Ensure team members are informed promptly and are available for immediate response.

2. **Roles and Responsibilities;**
   - Define and categorize the responsibilities of each team member during a crisis.
   - Example: Spokesperson handles external communications, Legal Representative assesses legal implications, Social Media Manager monitors and reports online conversations.

3. **Communication Protocols;**
   - Establish clear protocols for internal and external communication during a crisis.
   - Define channels, frequency of updates, and approval processes for crisis messages.

Response Actions

1. **Pre-drafted Crisis Messages;**
   - Develop pre-drafted crisis messages for various scenarios.
   - Create messages to address potential issues while maintaining credibility and transparency.

2. **Spokesperson Engagement;**
   - Designate a trained spokesperson for media interactions.
   - Coordinate with the Communications Specialist for external communication.

3. **Legal Consultation;**
   - Consult with the Legal Representative to ensure responses comply with legal requirements.
   - Assess potential legal risks and implications.

Post-Crisis Actions

1. **Recovery Strategy;**
   - Develop a strategy for rebuilding the organization's image post-crisis.
   - Communicate transparently, take corrective actions, and exhibit a commitment to improvement.

2. **Post-Crisis Review;**
   - Conduct a thorough review of the organization's response to identify lessons learned.

- ○ Update crisis response plans based on post-crisis evaluations.

Training and Simulation

1. **Regular Training;**
   - ○ Execute regular training sessions for the crisis management team and relevant staff.
   - ○ Ensure awareness of roles and procedures.

2. **Simulated Exercises:**
   - ○ Execute simulated crisis exercises to test the effectiveness of response plans.
   - ○ Evaluate team coordination and identify areas for improvement.

This Social Media Crisis Response Plan is to be reviewed annually and updated as needed.

Document Owner: [Crisis Manager]

Date of Last Revision: [Effective Date]

Pre-Drafted Crisis Messages Template

Objective

These pre-drafted crisis messages are designed to provide a prompt and consistent response to potential social media crises.

[Customize these messages based on the specific scenario, ensuring transparency, empathy, and commitment to resolution]

Product Quality Concerns

Context: Customer complaints about product quality on social media.

Crisis Message:

Dear [Customer Name],

We sincerely apologize for any inconvenience caused by your experience with our product. Your satisfaction is our priority, and we're actively working on the issue. Our customer support team will reach out to you shortly to gather more details and resolve this matter promptly. Thank you for bringing this to our attention.

Best regards,
[Your Company]

Data Breach Incident

Context: **Discovery of a potential data breach affecting customer information.**

Crisis Message:

Dear [Customer Name],

We regret to inform you that we have identified a potential data security incident. We take this matter very seriously and we are diligently working to solve and address the situation. Our IT team is implementing additional security measures, and we will keep you updated on our progress. If you have concerns or questions, please contact our dedicated support line at [Contact Number].

Sincerely,
[Your Company]

Service Interruption

Context: Reports of service interruptions causing inconvenience to customers.

Crisis Message:

Dear [Customer Name],

We understand the frustration caused by the recent service interruption. Our technical team is actively working to resolve the issue and will restore normal service. We appreciate your patience and understanding. We apologize for any inconvenience this may have caused. Updates on the resolution progress will be provided shortly.

Thank you for your understanding,
[Your Company]

Employee Conduct Issue

Context: Negative social media attention regarding employee conduct.

Crisis Message:

Dear [Customer Name],

We are aware of recent concerns raised about the conduct of one of our employees. We take such matters seriously and we are conducting a thorough investigation. Appropriate actions will be taken based on our findings. We sincerely apologize for any distress caused and assure you that this does not reflect our company's values.

Sincerely,
[Your Company]

Environmental Impact Concerns

Context: Allegations of environmental impact due to company practices.

Crisis Message:

Dear [Community/Customers],
We hear and share your concerns regarding the recent environmental impact allegations. We take these matters seriously and we are conducting a comprehensive review of our practices. Our commitment to sustainability remains resolute, and we will implement necessary changes to address these concerns. Regular updates will be provided as we take corrective actions.

Thank you for holding us accountable,
[Your Company]

Create these messages to fit the specific details of each context or scenario and maintain open lines of communication for ongoing updates and resolution.

Post-Crisis Image Rebuilding Strategy

Assessment and Reflection

1. Post-Crisis Review: Execute a thorough review of the crisis and analyze what went wrong, lessons learnt, and areas for improvement.

2. Stakeholder Feedback: Seek feedback from stakeholders, including customers, employees, and the public, to understand their perceptions and expectations moving forward.

Transparent Communication

1. Acknowledgment and Apology: Acknowledge the impact of the crisis publicly and issue an apology for any harm caused.

2. Transparency in Findings: Share key findings from the post-crisis review transparently, demonstrating accountability and a commitment to learning from the experience.

Corrective Actions

1. Immediate Corrective Measures: Carry out immediate corrective actions to address the root causes of the crisis and prevent similar incidents in the future.

2. Investment in Resources: Allocate resources to areas that need improvement, either in technology, employee training, or process enhancements.

3. Engage External Experts: Bring in external experts if necessary to carry out independent assessments and provide recommendations for improvement.

Employee Engagement and Training

1. Employee Communication: Develop open communication with employees, keeping them informed about the organization's commitment.

2. Training Programs: Carry out training programs to enhance employee skills and awareness, especially in areas related to the crisis.

Rebuilding Trust

1. Consistent Brand Messaging: Reinforce consistent brand messaging that expresses and reflects the organization's values, commitment to improvement and dedication to regaining trust.

2. Community Engagement: Engage actively with the affected community through initiatives, partnerships, or community service and demonstrate a commitment to giving back.

3. Social Responsibility Initiatives: Launch social responsibility initiatives that aligns with the organization's values, displaying a dedication to making a positive impact.

Continuous Improvement Culture

1. Feedback Mechanisms: Establish feedback mechanisms to encourage ongoing input from stakeholders.

2. Adaptive Strategy: cultivate an adaptive strategy that enables the organization to respond quickly to changing circumstances and evolving stakeholder expectations.

Communication Channels

1. Multichannel Approach: use a multichannel approach to communicate the organization's commitment to improvement, including official statements, press releases, and social media updates.

2. Interactive Platforms: Utilize interactive platforms, such as town hall meetings or virtual forums, to directly engage with stakeholders and address concerns.

Measurement and Reporting

1. Key Performance Indicators (KPIs): Clarity KPIs to measure progress in rebuilding the organization's image and regaining trust over time.

2.   Regular Reporting: Regularly provide reports on the status of improvement initiatives, emphasizing transparency and accountability.

By implementing this post-crisis image rebuilding strategy, your organization can demonstrate a genuine commitment

Tools for Social Listening

1. **Brandwatch:** Real-time   monitoring,   sentiment analysis, trend tracking.
   - ➤ It helps understand how the public perceives the brand post-crisis, identify emerging trends, and monitor sentiment changes.

2. **Hootsuite:** Social   media   monitoring,   sentiment analysis, custom analytics.
   - ➤ It helps track mentions across different social platforms, gauge sentiment, and measure the impact of communication strategies on public perception.

3. **Talkwalker:** Social   listening,   crisis   management, sentiment analysis.
   - ➤ It helps monitor online conversations, assess sentiment, and receive real-time alerts to address any arising issues swiftly.

4. **Sprout Social:** Social listening, sentiment analysis, trend analysis.

> It helps gain insights into post-crisis sentiment, track brand mentions, and recognize areas for improvement based on ongoing conversations.

5. **Meltwater:** Media monitoring, sentiment analysis, crisis management tools.
   > It helps monitor media coverage, analyze sentiment, and receive actionable insights to guide post-crisis communication techniques.

6. **Nuvi:** Social listening, sentiment analysis, crisis tracking.
   > It helps to monitor sentiment trends post-crisis, track online conversations, and gather insights for ongoing reputation management.

7. **Sysomos:** Social listening, sentiment analysis, crisis monitoring.
   > It helps understand public sentiment, track conversations around the brand, and assess the benefit of post-crisis communication strategies.

8. **Social Lakers:** Social listening, sentiment analysis, competitor benchmarking.
   > It helps monitor sentiment changes, benchmark against competitors, and adapt communication strategies based on ongoing public conversations.

9. **Brand24:** Social listening, sentiment analysis, real-time alerts.
   > It helps stay informed about public sentiment, receive instant alerts, and adapt communication techniques based on real-time data.

These social listening tools can provide organizations with the capability to monitor public sentiment, track ongoing conversations, and adjust their post-crisis strategies in response to emerging trends and feedback.

Chapter 11

MANAGING YOUR TIME ON SOCIAL MEDIA

Social media has become an essential part of our lives, with people spending hours every day scrolling through their feeds. While social media can be a source of entertainment and connection, it can also be a time-consuming distraction that takes away from more productive and effective activities. So, below are tips for managing your time on social media

1. Decide how much time you want to spend on social media each day and stick to it. Use a timer or app to help you track your usage and stop you from going over your limit.

2. Rather than mindlessly scrolling through your feed, follow accounts that encourage you, provide value, or help you learn something new. This will make your time on social media more productive and enriching.

3. Social media is a two-way street, so make sure you engage with others by commenting, liking, and sharing

their content. This will help you build connections and grow your network.

4. Social media notifications can be distracting and can disrupt your workflow. Turn off notifications for social media apps and check them only during designated times.

5. Social media can be a powerful tool for networking, learning, and growing your business. Instead of using it solely for entertainment, use it to connect with like-minded individuals, share your expertise, and promote your brand.

6. It's important to take breaks from social media to avoid burnout and maintain your mental health. Take time to detach from social media and engage in activities that bring you joy and peace.

Strategies for Maximizing Social Media Impact Without Sacrificing Productivity

1. Establish clear and specific goals for your social media activity, and prioritize the platforms and activities that will help you achieve those goals.

2. Develop a content calendar that outlines the topics and themes you want to cover, as well as the timing and frequency of your posts. Use scheduling tools to automate the process and save time.

3. Instead of trying to post constantly, focus on creating high-quality content that resonates with your audience. This will help you build a more engaged following and reduce the need for frequent posting.

4. Set aside specific times each day or week to engage with your followers and respond to comments and messages. Use tools like social listening to monitor conversations and identify opportunities to engage.

5. Track your social media metrics to understand what content is resonating with your audience and adjust your strategy accordingly. This will help you maximize your impact and ensure that your efforts are producing results.

6. Consider outsourcing certain aspects of your social media activity, such as content creation or management, to a third-party provider. This can free up your time and enable you to focus on other aspects of your business.

7. Set boundaries and limit the time you spend on social media to avoid getting sidetracked by endless scrolling and notifications. Use tools like website blockers or time management apps to stay focused and productive.

Tips for Staying Organized and Focused

1. **Make a to-do list:** Write down everything you need to do and prioritize the tasks. This will help you stay focused on what needs to be done and prevent you from getting distracted by less important tasks.

2. **Set goals:** Set clear, achievable goals for yourself and break them down into smaller, more manageable tasks. This will help you stay focused on what you want to achieve and give you a sense of accomplishment as you complete each task.

3. **Use a planner or calendar**: Keep track of your schedule and deadlines using a planner or calendar. This will help you stay organized and ensure that you don't miss any important appointments or deadlines.

4. **Minimize distractions**: Eliminate distractions as much as possible, such as turning off your phone or closing unnecessary tabs on your computer. This will help you stay focused on the task at hand and get it done more efficiently.

5. **Take breaks:** Take regular breaks to recharge your energy and prevent burnout. This will enable you to stay focused and productive throughout the day.

6. **Prioritize self-care:** Make sure to prioritize your physical and mental health by getting enough sleep, eating healthy, and exercising regularly. When you feel good physically and mentally, you'll be better equipped to stay organized and focused.

Outsourcing and Delegating Social Media Tasks

Outsourcing is the process of hiring a third-party company or individual to accomplish tasks or services for your business. Outsourcing can be a cost-effective way to access specialized skills, reduce operational costs, and increase efficiency.

Delegating social media tasks refers to the process of assigning specific social media-related responsibilities to other individuals or departments within your organization. This can include tasks such as creating social media content, managing social media accounts, monitoring social media activity, and analyzing social media metrics.

Outsourcing and delegating social media tasks can be an effective strategy for businesses of all sizes. By outsourcing or delegating these tasks, companies can free up internal resources and focus on core competencies while still maintaining a strong social media presence. However, it is important to carefully select and monitor the individuals or companies that are handling your social media tasks to ensure they align with your brand and meet your expectations.

Outsourcing and delegating social media tasks can be a great way to save time and resources, while also ensuring that your social media presence remains active and engaging. Here are few tips for outsourcing and delegating social media tasks:

1. **Identify which tasks to outsource:** Start by identifying which tasks you want to outsource or delegate. This could include tasks such as content creation, scheduling posts, responding to comments and messages, and analyzing social media metrics.

2. **Find the right person or team:** Look for a qualified and experienced person or team to handle your social media tasks. This could be a social media manager, a freelancer, or a social media agency. Make sure to check their references, portfolio, and social media profiles to ensure that they have the necessary skills and experience.

3. **Set clear goals and expectations:** Clearly communicate your goals and expectations to the person or team handling your social media tasks. This should include guidelines for tone of voice, content themes, and posting frequency. Provide them with any relevant brand guidelines or style guides, as well as access to any necessary tools or platforms.

4. **Monitor progress and provide feedback:** Regularly monitor the progress of your social media tasks and provide feedback to the person or team handling them. This will help ensure that they are meeting your goals and expectations, and allow you to make any necessary adjustments.

5. **Stay involved:** While outsourcing and delegating social media tasks can save you time and resources, it's important to stay involved in the process. Make sure to regularly review the content being posted, engage with your audience, and provide input and feedback as needed.

By following these tips, you can find the right person or team to handle your social media tasks, set clear goals and expectations, and monitor progress to ensure that you are meeting your social media goals.

Chapter 12

LEADING BY EXAMPLE

Leading by example is a leadership style where a leader sets a positive example for their team members by modeling the behavior they want to see.

1. **Be a role model**: As a leader, you should set an example by demonstrating the behavior you want your team members to exhibit. This includes traits such as integrity, accountability, and a strong work ethic.

2. **Communicate clearly:** Effective communication is a key component of leading by example. Make sure to clearly communicate your expectations and goals, and provide regular feedback to your team members.

3. **Be proactive**: Take a proactive approach to problem-solving and decision-making. This will demonstrate to your team members that you are committed to finding solutions and making things happen.

4. **Practice what you preach:** Don't just talk the talk – make sure to follow through on your commitments and promises. This will demonstrate to your team members that you are reliable and trustworthy.

5. **Celebrate successes**: Make sure to recognize and celebrate your team's successes. This will help to build morale and reinforce positive behaviors.

6. **Continuously learn and grow**: As a leader, you should be committed to continuous learning and growth. This will demonstrate to your team members that you are dedicated to improving your skills and abilities.

Leading by example is an effective leadership style that can inspire and motivate team members to follow suit. By modeling positive behavior, communicating clearly, being proactive, practicing what you preach, celebrating successes, and continuously learning and growing, you can set a positive example for your team members and create a culture of excellence.

The Importance of CEO Leadership in Social Media Management

CEO leadership is crucial in social media management because it sets the tone for the organization's overall social media strategy and messaging. As the leader of the company, the CEO has a significant influence on how the company is perceived by the public, and this extends to the organization's social media presence.

Here are some reasons why CEO leadership is important in social media management:

1. **Establishing a clear brand voice:** The CEO is responsible for defining the organization's values, mission, and vision. These elements are critical in developing a consistent brand voice, which is essential for effective social media management. The CEO's leadership can ensure that the organization's messaging across all social media platforms aligns with the company's overall brand voice.

2. **Creating a culture of transparency:** In today's world, consumers expect transparency from the companies they engage with on social media. The CEO can set the tone for the organization by promoting a culture of transparency and openness. By leading by example, the CEO can encourage the rest of the organization to be honest and transparent in their social media interactions with customers.

3. **Demonstrating thought leadership**: The CEO can use social media to establish themselves and the organization as thought leaders in their industry. By sharing insights and perspectives on industry trends, the CEO can help the organization gain credibility and build trust with customers and stakeholders.

4. **Responding to crises**: In the event of a social media crisis, the CEO's leadership is critical in managing the situation. By providing clear guidance and direction, the

CEO can help the organization navigate the crisis and protect its reputation.

Embracing Ongoing Learning and Growth in Social Media Management

Embracing ongoing learning and growth is important for social media managers to stay up-to-date with the constantly evolving social media landscape.

1. **Stay informed:** Stay up-to-date with the latest social media trends, news, and best practices. This can be done by following industry leaders and influencers, attending conferences and webinars, reading blogs and articles, and subscribing to newsletters and podcasts.

2. **Experiment and test**: Experiment with different types of content, platforms, and strategies. Test different tactics and measure the results to determine what works best for your audience and goals.

3. **Seek feedback:** Seek feedback from your team, colleagues, and followers to gain insights into what they like and what they want to see more of. Use this feedback to adjust your strategy and improve your content.

4. **Learn from others**: Learn from other social media managers and organizations. Engage with them on social media, participate in online communities, and attend networking events.

5. **Take courses and certifications**: Take courses and certifications to develop new skills and enhance your knowledge. Many universities and online platforms offer social media courses and certifications, including Facebook Blueprint, Twitter Flight School, and Hootsuite Academy.

6. **Develop a growth mindset:** Adopt a growth mindset and be open to learning and trying new things. Embrace challenges and mistakes as opportunities to learn and improve.

By embracing ongoing learning and growth, social media managers can stay ahead of the curve and develop the skills and knowledge needed to succeed in the dynamic world of social media.

Chapter 13

THE 60-DAY SOCIAL CEO CHALLENGE

Welcome to your personal experience for social media mastery! This 60-day challenge is developed to guide you in transforming your understanding of social media into definite action and results. The challenge is divided into 12 weeks, with each focusing on a required aspect of building a thriving online presence. You'll find a mix of theoretical insights, practical activities, and reflection prompts to keep you engaged and on track

Week 1: Set Goals and Define Your Strategy

☐ **Day 1:** Read and familiarize yourself with the book "THE SOCIAL CEO".

☐ **Day 2-3:** Set clear social media goals for your business.

☐ **Day 4-5:** Define your social media strategy, including target audience, platforms, and content types.

Week 2-3: Create and Curate Content

☐ **Day 6-8:** Create a content calendar for the next 30 days, including themes, topics, and publishing schedule.

☐ **Day 9-10:** Research and curate industry-related content to share on your social media channels.

☐ **Day 11-12:** Create and schedule at least two weeks' worth of social media posts.

Week 4-5: Engage with Your Audience

☐ **Day 13-15:** Develop a plan for responding to comments, messages, and reviews on your social media channels.

☐ **Day 16-18**: Start engaging with your audience by responding to comments and messages and participating in relevant conversations.

☐ **Day 19-20:** Plan and execute a social media campaign to increase engagement and reach.

Week 6-7: Analyze and Optimize Your Strategy

☐ **Day 21-24:** Set up social media analytics and tracking tools to monitor your performance.

☐ **Day 25-27:** Analyze your social media metrics and identify areas for improvement.

☐ **Day 28-30:** Optimize your social media strategy based on your analysis, including content types, posting schedule, and audience targeting.

Week 8-9: Expand Your Reach

☐ **Day 31-34:** Identify influencers and partners in your industry and plan a collaboration or partnership.

☐ **Day 35-37**: Explore paid social media advertising options to increase your reach.

☐ **Day 38-40:** Plan and execute a social media contest or giveaway to attract new followers and engagement.

Week 10-11: Monitor Your Reputation and Crisis Management

☐ **Day 41-44:** Develop a plan for monitoring your brand's reputation on social media.

☐ **Day 45-47:** Plan and practice crisis management procedures for negative reviews or social media backlash.

☐ **Day 48-50:** Regularly monitor your social media channels for any potential issues or negative feedback.

Week 12: Evaluate and Adjust

☐ **Day 51-54:** Evaluate your social media strategy and results over the past 60 days.

☐ **Day 55-57:** Make any necessary adjustments to your strategy, goals, or tactics.

☐ **Day 58-60:** Create a long-term plan for social media management and continue to monitor and adjust your strategy accordingly.

Consistency is key. Commit to daily and weekly engagement with your online community, even if it's merely for a few minutes. This sustained step will gradually build your authority, attract engaged followers, and eventually contribute to your business's success. Effective social media management requires ongoing effort and dedication. By following this 60-day exercise and challenge, you can establish a strong foundation for your business's social media presence and set yourself up for long-term success.

APPENDIX

Case Studies of CEOs and Social Media Success

- **Gary Vaynerchuk (CEO of VaynerMedia and creator of Veefriends):** A pioneer in digital marketing, Gary's personal brand on platforms like Twitter and YouTube has fueled the growth of his agency. His authenticity, actionable advice, and engaging personality attract millions of followers, leading to speaking engagements, book deals, and brand partnerships.

- **Satya Nadella (CEO of Microsoft):** Nadella transformed Microsoft's image by actively engaging on LinkedIn and Twitter. He showcases company culture, celebrates employee achievements, and fosters open communication with stakeholders. This accessibility and vulnerability have contributed to Microsoft's renewed relevance and optimistic brand perception.

- **Reshma Saujani (CEO of Mom's_first_US and Girls Who Code):** Through Twitter and Instagram, Saujani shares her organization's mission of closing the gender gap in tech. Her personal stories, inspirational quotes, and

156

behind-the-scenes glances into Girls Who Code events engage supporters and attract partnerships, advancing the organization's reach and impact.

- **Tony Hsieh (Former CEO of Zappos):** The late Hsieh famously used Twitter to directly connect with customers, troubleshoot issues, and build a strong community around Zappos. His transparency and down-to-earth personality humanized the brand and fueled customer loyalty.

- **Jessica Alba (CEO of The Honest Company):** Jessica Alba leverages Instagram and YouTube to build trust and transparency with her brand of eco-friendly baby products. She shares parenting tips, product demonstrations, and behind-the-scenes glimpses into The Honest Company's mission which helps in creating a loyal customer base who connect with her values.

- **Elon Musk (CEO of Tesla & SpaceX):** While often controversial, Musk's Twitter presence is undeniable in its impact. His bold statements, technical insights, and even memes fuel media coverage and brand awareness for Tesla and SpaceX. While this approach carries risks, it has undoubtedly contributed to his companies' visibility and growth.

- **Arianna Huffington (CEO of HuffPost):** Huffington used Twitter and LinkedIn to amplify HuffPost's content and engage with influential figures. Her thought leadership on topics like sleep and well-being resonated with readers, boosting traffic and establishing her as a prominent voice in the media.

- **Blake Mycoskie (CEO of TOMS):** Mycoskie is a CEO who uses social media to directly connect with customers and share the story behind TOMS' "One for One" model. His Instagram and Facebook stories showcase volunteer trips, customer contributions, and the impact of TOMS shoes on children in need, leading to brand loyalty and increased customer engagement.

- **Tim Cook (CEO of Apple):** While less vocal than some on social media, Cook's use of Twitter focuses on highlighting Apple's values, environmental initiatives, and product launches. His measured voice and focus on company news contribute to Apple's image as a leader in innovation and responsible tech.

- **Lisa Su (CEO of AMD):** Su has used Twitter and LinkedIn to connect with gamers, tech enthusiasts, and investors. Her technical expertise, transparency on company strategy, and engagement with the gaming community have fueled AMD's resurgence in the chip market and created a better relatable brand image.

These are just a few examples of CEOs who have successfully leveraged social media to benefit their businesses. By focusing on various industries and company sizes, we see the various ways social media can be used to build brand awareness, engage with customers, and drive business growth.

Tools and Resources for Social Media Management

Scheduling Platforms
- Hootsuite
- Buffer
- Sendible
- Sprout Social
- Later

Analytics Dashboards
- Hootsuite Analytics
- Sprout Social Analytics
- Buffer Analyze
- Socialbakers
- Brandwatch

Image Editing Tools
- **Canva:** For creating social media graphics, banners, stories, and videos with templates
- **Adobe Photoshop:** For professional photo editing, manipulation, and graphic design.
- **Adobe Spark:** Photo and video editing for creating professional-looking social media content.
- **Snapseed:** For powerful and convenient photo editing with features like filters, adjustments and selective editing
- **Stencil:** For creating social media images with pre-designed templates, icons, and text overlays.

Keyword Research Resources
- ➤ Google Keyword Planner
- ➤ Ahrefs
- ➤ SEMrush
- ➤ Buzzsumo
- ➤ Socialbakers' Hashtag Research

Bonus Resources:
- **Unsplash:** Free stock photo library with high-quality images.
- **Pexels:** Free stock photo library with curated collections and diverse visuals.
- **Grammarly:** Grammar and plagiarism checker for crafting clear and error-free social media content.
- **Copysmith:** AI-powered tool for generating creative social media captions and ad copy.
- **HubSpot Academy:** Offers free online courses and resources on social media marketing, content creation, and analytics.

These are just a few of the many valuable tools and resources available for social media management. The best tools for you will depend on your specific needs and budget. Research and try them out to find the platforms that work best for you and your business.

500 SOCIAL MEDIA TIPS

Social Media Strategy

1. Define clear, measurable goals for your social media action.
2. Create a content calendar to maintain consistency.
3. Embrace video content for increased engagement.
4. Leverage user-generated content for authenticity.
5. Tailor content to your target audience's preferences and behaviors.

Content Creation

6. Prioritize quality over quantity in your content.
7. Create shareable and visually attractive graphics.
8. Use storytelling to connect with your audience emotionally.
9. Incorporate trending and relevant hashtags.
10. Try out diverse content formats (images, videos, infographics)

Audience Engagement

11. Respond promptly to comments, messages, and mentions.
12. Foster user participation through contests and challenges.
13. Host live sessions for real-time interaction.
14. Collaborate with influencers to expand your reach.
15. Build a community by acknowledging and thanking your audience.

Analytics and Optimization

16. Conduct A/B testing for ad creatives and copy.
18. Optimize posting times based on audience activity.
19. Monitor performance of individual posts to refine strategy.
19. Adapt and adjust strategies based on insights and feedback.
20. Analysis social media analytics regularly.

Platform-Specific Tips

21. Leverage Instagram Stories for behind-the-scenes content.
22. Create visually attractive and informative Pins for Pinterest.
23. Use Twitter polls to engage and gather audience ideas.
24. Try out short-form video content on TikTok.
25. Use LinkedIn for B2B marketing and proficient networking.

Paid Advertising

26. Target specific demographics with paid ads.
27. Use retargeting ads to reach users who visited your website.
28. Test various ad placements for optimal performance.
29. Set a budget and bid strategy aligned with your objectives.
30. Monitor ad relevance scores and adjust as needed.

Community Building

31. Cultivate a sense of community by enabling discussions.
32. Create Facebook Groups centered around shared interests.
33. Highlight and celebrate user milestones or accomplishments.
34. Share user testimonials and success stories.
35. Humanize your brand by showcasing the faces behind it.

Innovative Content Ideas

36. Share behind-the-scenes glances of your work process.
37. Create interactive quizzes or polls to engage your audience.
38. Feature employee spotlights to add a unique touch.
39. Create infographics to disseminate complex information.
40. Host virtual events or webinars to provide value.

Consistency and Timing

41. Post consistently to maintain a regular presence.
42. Schedule posts during peak engagement periods.
43. Evaluate time zone differences for a global audience.
44. Design themed content for special occasions or holidays.
45. Share industry news and updates to remain relevant.

Storytelling Techniques

46. Craft compelling narratives to evoke sentiments.
47. Share customer success stories to build trust.
48. Use the hero's journey framework for brand storytelling.
49. Share your brand's journey, challenges, and growth.
50. Implement episodic content for ongoing engagement.

SEO for Social Media

51. Optimize your profiles with relevant keywords.
52. Use explanatory/descriptive captions and alt text for images.
53. Use trending and niche hashtags.
54. Share user-generated content(UGC) with appropriate tags.
55. Leverage geo-tags for location-specific visibility.

Employee Advocacy

56. Employees should share company content on their profiles.
57. Feature employee takeovers on social media.
58. Showcase workplace culture through employee perspectives.
59. Enforce an employee advocacy program for amplification.
60. Acknowledge and celebrate employee achievements publicly.

Visual Storytelling

61. Use Instagram and Facebook carousels for storytelling.
62. Create visually consistent branding across platforms.
63. Use aesthetically pleasing visuals to capture attention.
64. Try out cinemagraphs or animated graphics.
65. Integrate user-generated images to humanize your brand.

User Experience (UX) Focus

66. Optimize your profile bio and about sections for clarity.
67. Provide easy navigation and a seamless user experience.
68. Regularly test your website and social media links.
69. Use clear CTAs (Call-to-Actions) in your posts.
70. Monitor and respond to customer feedback promptly.

Story Highlights

71. Use Instagram and Facebook story highlights effectively.
72. Classify story highlights for easy navigation.
73. Regularly update and refresh your story highlights.
74. Use eye-catching cover images for each highlight.
75. Showcase products and services in highlights.

Employee-generated Content

76. Encourage employees to share their work experiences.
77. Feature employee-generated content on your official channels.
78. Create a designated hashtag for employee content.
79. Acknowledge and appreciate employee contributions publicly.
80. Use employee content to showcase company culture.

Authenticity and Transparency

81. Share authentic moments (I.e; behind challenges or mistakes)
82. Be transparent about your brand values and mission.
83. Feature behind-the-scenes content to humanize your brand.
84. React openly to criticism or negative feedback.
85. Showcase the faces and personalities behind your brand.

Podcasting and Audio Content

86. Start a podcast to share industry insights and conversations.
87. Share snippets or highlights from podcast episodes.
88. Use audio content for Q&A sessions or interviews.
89. Optimize your podcast for different platforms.
90. Cross-promote podcast episodes on social media.

Social Responsibility Initiatives

91. Bring out your brand's commitment to social causes.
92. Share updates on charitable donations or partnerships.

93. Involve your audience in philanthropic industries.
94. Integrate sustainability practices and share them.
95. Use social media to bring up awareness about important issues.

Interactive Content

96. Create interactive polls or quizzes on Instagram and Facebook.
97. Host live Q&A sessions for real-time engagement.
98. Use interactive elements like sliders or emoji reactions.
99. Perform social media challenges or contests.
100. Try out augmented reality (AR) filters.

Influencer Collaborations

101. Identify influencers aligned with your brand values.
102. Establish real and genuine relationships with influencers.
103. Collaborate on co-created content for authenticity.
104. Use influencer reach to tap into new audiences.
105. Estimate the impact of influencer collaborations.

Custom GIFs and Stickers

106. Create custom GIFs and stickers for Instagram and other platforms.
107. Use branded GIFs to improve visual storytelling.
108. Encourage users to create content using your GIFs.
109. Leverage GIFs for playful, enjoyable and engaging content.
110. Monitor the performance of branded GIFs.

Accessibility and Inclusivity

111. Add alt text to images for accessibility.
112. Ensure captions are available for video content.
113. Use inclusive words or language in your posts.
114. Share content that reflects various perspectives.
115. Audit your content regularly for exclusivity

Personal Branding

116. Develop a consistent personal brand on social media.
117. Share your professional journey and expertise.
118. Use a consistent tone and style in your posts.
119. Engage with your audience authentically.
120. Leverage your personal brand for networking.

Online Events and Webinars

121. Host virtual events or webinars for your audience.
122. Stimulate events through dedicated social media campaigns.
123. Use live Q&A sessions to interact with participants.
124. Share highlights and takeaways post-event.
125. Repurpose event content for ongoing engagement.

Strategic Use of Emojis

126. Integrate emojis to add personality to your posts.
127. Use emojis to emphasize key points in your captions.
128. Create branded emojis for a unique touch.
129. Ensure emojis align with your brand tone.
130. Monitor and observe audience reactions to different emojis.

Industry Partnerships

131. Explore partnerships with other brands in your industry.
132. Collaborate on mutual campaigns or projects.
133. Cross-promote each other's content.
134. Tap into shared audiences for mutual benefit.
135. Estimate the impact of industry partnerships.

Social Media Contests

136. Host engaging contests to stimulate user participation.
137. Set clear rules and deadlines for contests.
138. Use contests to generate user-generated content.
139. Offer attractive prizes to incentivize participation.
140. Promote contests across different channels.

Content Repurposing

141. Repurpose successful content for various platforms.
142. Convert blog posts into visually appealing infographics.
143. Create video snippets from longer-form content.
144. Share throwback content to evoke nostalgia.
145. Monitor engagement metrics for repurposed content.

User Surveys and Polls

146. Conduct user surveys to gather feedback.
147. Use polls to gauge audience opinions.
148. Implement feedback from surveys to make improvement.
149. Share insights from polls and surveys.
150. Showcase changes made based on user feedback.

Behind-the-Scenes Content

151. Share behind-the-scenes content to humanize your brand.
152. Provide glances into your workspace or creative process.
153. Bring out the dedication of your team members.
154. Create a series of behind-the-scenes stories or posts.
155. Show the personality behind your brand.

Guest Posts and Takeovers

156. Cooperate with influencers/industry experts for guest posts.
157. Host Instagram takeovers for a fresh perspective.
158. Feature guest bloggers on your website or blog.
159. Cross-promote guest content on different channels.
160. Ensure alignment with your brand values.

Adopt Ephemeral Content

161. UseInstagram and Facebook Stories for timely updates.
162. Share limited-time offers or flash sales via Stories.
163. Use Stories for exclusive behind-the-scenes moments.
164. Try out Instagram Reels or Snapchat Snaps.
165. Leverage the urgency of ephemeral content.

Interactive Quizzes and Games

166. Create interactive quizzes related to your industry/products.
167. Host trivia games to engage your audience.
168. Integrate gamification elements in your content.
169. Reward participants or winners with shoutouts or prizes.
170. Make learning about your brand enjoyable.

Memes and Humor

171. Infuse humor into your content with relevant memes.

172. Create branded memes that resonate with your audience.

173. Stay updated on trending memes and adapt them.

174. Be mindful of cultural sensitivity when using humor.

175. Use humor to connect with your audience authentically.

LinkedIn Engagement Strategies

176. Share thought leadership content on LinkedIn.

177. Take part in relevant LinkedIn Groups for networking.

178. Use LinkedIn Live for real-time engagement.

179. Optimize your LinkedIn profile for professional visibility.

180. Showcase company achievements and updates.

Curated Content

181. Curate content from industry leaders or publications.

182. Share curated content that aligns with your brand voice.

183. Provide insights or opinions when sharing curated content.

184. Mention and tag the original creators for credit.

185. Offer a combination of original and curated content.

Seasonal and Trend Integration

186. Align your content with current seasons or holidays.

187. Monitor trending topics and integrate them judiciously.

188. Use relevant hashtags related to ongoing trends.

189. Create content that reflects seasonal themes.

190. Stay agile and adapt content based on emerging trends.

In-App Features Exploration

191. Explore new features within social media platforms.
192. Use stickers, filters, and augmented reality (AR) effects.
193. Try out platform-specific video features.
194. Stay updated on platform information and updates.
195. Showcase creativity using the latest features.

Customer Spotlights

196. Feature customer success stories on your social media.
197. Highlight customer testimonials or reviews.
198. Encourage customers to share their experiences.
199. Create a dedicated series for customer spotlights.
200. Express gratitude for customer loyalty.

User-Generated Content (UGC)

201. Encourage users to create content related to your brand.
202. Create an hashtag for gathering user-generated content.
203. Showcase user-generated content on your official channels.
204. Run UGC contests or challenges to boost participation.
205. Express appreciation to users for their contributions.

Infographics for Informational Content

206. Design infographic for disseminating complex information.
207. Use visually appealing charts and graphs in infographics.
208. Share infographics across platforms for engagement.
209. Create step-by-step guides using infographic format.
210. Monitor engagement metrics for infographic performance.

Collaborative Projects

211. Collaborate with other brands or creators on projects.
212. Co-create content that brings unique value to audiences.
213. Promote collaborative projects on each other's channels.
214. Leverage combined audiences for broader reach.
215. Ensure synergy and alignment in collaborative efforts.

Diversify Content Formats

216. Try out different content formats.
217. Integrate video content into your strategy.
218. Create shareable and visually appealing images.
219. Use carousels for a sequential storytelling approach.
220. Maintain a balance between text, visuals, and multimedia.

Promotional Strategies

221. Plan strategic promotions aligned with business goals.
222. Create limited-time offers or flash sales for urgency.
223. Leverage social media ads for targeted promotions.
224. Integrate promo codes or exclusive discounts in posts.
225. Monitor ROI and adjust promotional strategies accordingly.

Educational Webinars or Tutorials

226. Host educational webinars or tutorial sessions.
227. Share valuable insights and knowledge.
228. Use live sessions for real-time engagement.
229. Create teaser content to promote upcoming webinars.
230. Foster audience questions and interaction.

Cross-Platform Consistency

231. Maintain consistency in branding across all platforms.
232. Ensure uniform profile images and bios.
233. Align content tone and style across all channels.
234. Use cross-promotion to direct traffic between platforms.
235. Monitor analytics for platform-specific performance.

Localized Content

236. Create content to appeal to specific geographic locations.
237. Use location-based hashtags to reach local audiences.
238. Highlight community events or partnerships.
239. Engage with local influencers or businesses.
240. Showcase the human side of your brand.

Testimonial Videos

241. Request customers to create video testimonials.
242. Showcase authentic customer experiences.
243. Edit videos for concise and impactful storytelling.
244. Use video testimonials in marketing campaigns.
245. Express gratitude to customers for their contributions.

Email List Integration

246. Promote newsletter sign-ups through social media.
247. Share exclusive content or offers for subscribers.
248. Use social media to drive traffic to your website.
249. Segment email lists based on social media engagement.
250. Analyze conversion rates from social media referrals.

Interactive Virtual Events

251. Host virtual events with interactive elements.
252. Use chat features for audience engagement.
253. Offer virtual networking opportunities.
254. Share highlights and key takeaways post-event.
255. Integrate social media for event promotion.

Storytelling Techniques

256. Use storytelling to convey brand narratives.
257. Create relatable and emotionally vibrant stories.
258. Share success stories or milestones in your journey.
259. Use Instagram and Facebook Story features.
260. Monitor audience responses to storytelling content.

Dynamic Content Scheduling

261. Try out different posting times.
262. Use scheduling tools for consistent posting.
263. Adjust posting frequency based on audience activity.
264. Leverage analytics to identify peak engagement times.
265. Optimize content scheduling for different time zones.

Facebook Groups for Community Building

266. Create and manage a Facebook Group for your community.
267. Facilitate discussions, questions, and interactions.
268. Share exclusive content within the group.
269. Foster a sense of belonging and camaraderie.
270. Monitor group activity and address member needs.

Interactive User Polls

271. Use polls on Twitter, Instagram, or Facebook.
272. Gather feedback on potential product features.
273. Engage users with lighthearted or fun polls.
274. Share results and insights from user polls.
275. Adjust strategies based on user preferences.

Augmented Reality (AR) Filters

276. Create branded AR filters for Instagram and Facebook.
277. Encourage users to share content using your filters.
278. Promote filters as part of marketing campaigns.
279. Monitor usage and engagement with AR filters.
280. Update or launch new filters continuously.

Educational Series / Challenges

281. Develop an educational content series.
282. Break down complex topics into digestible segments.
283. Motivate audience participation through challenges.
284. Use dedicated hashtags for series or challenges.
285. Recognize and appreciate participants.

Social Media Analytics Mastery

286. Dive deep into analytics for each platform.
287. Identify top-performing content and replicate success.
288. Monitor audience demographics and behaviors.
289. Adjust strategies based on real-time analytics.
290. Use analytics for data-driven decision-making.

User Reviews and Testimonials

291. Respond to user reviews, including positive and negative.
292. Encourage satisfied customers to leave reviews.
293. Share positive testimonials on your social media channels.
294. Showcase user-generated content as social proof.
295. Address negative reviews with empathy and solutions.

Consistent Brand Messaging

296. Ensure your brand message aligns with company values.
297. Maintain consistency in tone and messaging.
298. Integrate brand messaging into visual elements.
299. Educate your audience about your brand ethos.
300. Use storytelling to strengthen brand identity.

Adaptability to Trends

301. Stay updated on arising social media trends.
302. Try out new formats and features.
303. Assess the relevance of trends to your brand.
304. Adapt content strategies based on evolving trends.
305. Balance trendiness with brand authenticity.

Accessibility and Inclusivity

306. Create content accessible to diverse audiences.
307. Use alt text for images and videos.
308. Consider readability for captions and text overlays.
309. Represent inclusivity in visuals and messaging.
310. Showcase your brand's commitment to diversity.

Strategic Hashtag Usage

311. Research and use trending and relevant hashtags.
312. Create branded hashtags for campaigns.
313. Avoid excessive or irrelevant hashtag use.
314. Monitor hashtag performance using analytics.
315. Boost user participation through hashtags.

Live Q&A Sessions

316. Host live Q&A sessions to engage with your audience.
317. Collect questions in advance for better organization.
318. Handle inquiries about products, services, or industry.
319. Use live sessions to humanize your brand.
320. Thank participants for their questions and engagement.

Localized Influencer Collaborations

321. Collaborate with influencers in specific regions.
322. Use influencers to reach local audiences.
323. Ensure influencers resonate with local culture.
324. Leverage regional holidays or events in collaborations.
325. Evaluate the influencer's impact on regional engagement.

Engaging Caption Strategies

326. Craft compelling and concise captions.
327. Use storytelling elements in captions.
328. Pose questions to prompt audience interaction.
329. Incorporate emojis or symbols for visual appeal.
330. Create captions to suit the tone of each platform.

Adaptive Content Repurposing

331. Repurpose evergreen content for ongoing relevance.
332. Create content formats for different platforms.
333. Convert blog posts into engaging social media snippets.
334. Create visually appealing infographics from statistics.
335. Monitor engagement metrics for repurposed content.

Dynamic Carousel Posts

336. Use carousel posts for a sequential narrative.
337. Showcase product features in a carousel format.
338. Create step-by-step tutorials or guides.
339. Encourage users to swipe for more information.
340. Test different carousel post structures for effectiveness.

Interactive Contests or Challenges

341. Launch interactive contests or challenges.
342. Motivate user participation through creativity.
343. Align contests with your brand identity.
344. Offer appealing incentives or prizes.
345. Share user-generated content from the contest.

In-depth Industry Analysis

346. Perform thorough analyses of your industry landscape.
347. Monitor competitor strategies and performance.
348. Identify gaps in the market for unique possibilities.
349. Align your content with industry trends and shifts.
350. Share insights to position your brand as an industry leader.

Localized Advertising Campaigns

351. Create advertising campaigns for specific regions.
352. Use localized language and cultural references.
353. Highlight region-specific product benefits.
354. Monitor ad performance metrics across regions.
355. Optimize ads based on regional audience behaviors.

Customer-Centric Surveys

356. Conduct surveys to gather customer feedback.
357. Use surveys to understand preferences and pain points.
358. Share survey results with actionable insights.
359. Implement changes based on customer feedback.
360. Express gratitude for customers' valuable input.

Personalized Content Recommendations

361. Leverage data to offer personalized content.
362. Use algorithms to suggest products or content.
363. Implement user preference tracking for tailored suggestions.
364. Share personalized success stories or experiences.
365. Refine recommendations based on user interactions.

LinkedIn Publishing Platform

366. Use LinkedIn's publishing platform for long-form content.
367. Share industry insights, thought leadership, or case studies.
368. Leverage the platform's professional network for visibility.
369. Promote published articles across other social channels.
370. Engage with comments and build a professional network.

Seasonal Influencer Partnerships

371. Collaborate with influencers for seasonal campaigns.
372. Tailor content to align with seasonal themes.
373. Create limited-time collaborations for urgency.
374. Feature influencers in festive or themed content.
375. Express appreciation for influencer contributions.

Targeted Retargeting Campaigns

376. Implement retargeting campaigns for website visitors.
377. Create tailored content for specific audience segments.
378. Use retargeting to showcase abandoned cart items.
379. Monitor retargeting campaign effectiveness metrics.
380. Adjust strategies based on retargeting performance.

Inclusive Content Representation

381. Ensure diverse representation in visual content.
382. Showcase a range of demographics in imagery.
383. Collaborate with creators from diverse backgrounds.
384. Integrate inclusive language in your captions and copy.
385. Reflect a variety of perspectives in your content.
386. Engage in conversations around diversity and inclusion.
387. Assess and enhance your inclusivity efforts regularly.
388. Celebrate cultural events with respectful and authentic content.
389. Encourage feedback on inclusivity from your audience.
390. Showcase real stories that resonate with diverse experiences.

Regularly Updated FAQs

391. Maintain a comprehensive and up-to-date FAQ section.
392. Address common customer queries in your FAQs.
393. Use FAQs as a resource for customer support teams.
394. Promote your FAQs across social media for visibility.
395. Review and update FAQs regularly based on emerging questions.

Video Series for In-Depth Insights

396. Develop a video series for detailed insights.
397. Handle complex industry topics in video format.
398. Create a playlist for easy navigation and binge-watching.
399. Share teaser content to build anticipation.
400. Stimulate audience interaction through comments.

Diversified Story Formats

401. Try out different Instagram Story formats.
402. Use polls, quizzes, and countdowns for engagement.
403. Share behind-the-scenes content in Story Highlights.
404. Collaborate with followers through Story mentions.
405. Monitor Story analytics for performance insights.

Interactive Contests

406. Launch creative and interactive contests.
407. Encourage user-generated content with clear guidelines.
408. Leverage voting or judging mechanisms for fairness.
409. Feature contest entries on your social media.
410. Announce winners with appreciation for participation.

Industry Collaborations for Authority

411. Collaborate with recognized industry figures.
412. Feature guest posts or takeovers on your social channels.
413. Attend and cover industry events for real-time updates.
414. Share your perspective on industry developments.
415. Express gratitude for collaboration with industry leaders.

LinkedIn Company Pages

416. Optimize your LinkedIn Company Page for professionalism.
417. Regularly update your company's LinkedIn feed.
418. Showcase company achievements, milestones, and events.
419. Encourage employees to engage with company updates.
420. Utilize LinkedIn analytics to assess page performance.

Pinterest Strategy for Visual Brands

421. Create visually appealing Pins for Pinterest.
422. Use Pinterest boards to categorize content.
423. Integrate keyword-rich descriptions for searchability.
424. Share a mix of product-related and lifestyle Pins.
425. Monitor Pinterest analytics for popular Pins and trends.

Consistent Email Newsletter Schedule

426. Establish a consistent schedule for email newsletters.
427. Segment newsletters based on audience preferences.
428. Provide valuable content exclusive to newsletters.
429. Use newsletters to drive traffic to social media channels.
430. Analyze email open rates and adjust strategies accordingly.

Localized Challenges or Events

431. Launch challenges or events tailored to specific regions.
432. Incorporate local cultural elements in challenges.
433. Promote regional events or collaborations.
434. Use localized language and hashtags for engagement.
435. Share highlights and participant contributions.

YouTube Playlists for Content Organization

436. Organize your YouTube content into playlists.
437. Group videos based on themes or series.
438. Use playlists for easy navigation and binge-watching.
439. Share playlist links on other social media platforms.
440. Update playlists regularly with new content.

Interactive Customer Journey Map

441. Create an interactive customer journey map.
442. Highlight key touchpoints and decision-making stages.
443. Share customer success stories within the map.
444. Use visuals and graphics for a compelling presentation.
445. Monitor user interactions with the journey map.

Google My Business Optimization

446. Optimize your Google My Business listing.
447. Ensure accurate business information and categories.
448. Use Google Posts to share updates and offers.
449. Encourage customers to leave reviews on Google.
450. Review and respond to customer feedback regularly.

Twitter Chats for Community Engagement

451. Host Twitter chats to engage with your audience.
452. Choose relevant topics for Twitter chat discussions.
453. Use a designated hashtag for easy tracking.
454. Encourage participants to share insights and questions.
455. Share a recap or highlights post-chat.

AI-Enhanced Customer Service

456. Integrate AI tools for efficient customer service.
457. Use chatbots to address common queries.
458. Provide instant responses to customer inquiries.
459. Ensure seamless transition to human support when needed.
460. Monitor customer satisfaction with AI-driven interactions.

Share Industry Insights and Research

461. Share valuable industry insights and research findings.
462. Create visually appealing graphics for key statistics.
463. Provide actionable takeaways for your audience.
464. Collaborate with industry experts for joint research.
465. Encourage discussions around the presented insights.

Community Building on Discord

466. Create a Discord server for your community.
467. Foster real-time conversations and interactions.
468. Establish channels for different topics or interests.
469. Host AMAs (Ask Me Anything) sessions on Discord.
470. Appreciate active members and contributors.

Promote Employee Advocacy

471. Encourage employees to share company updates.
472. Provide employees with shareable content assets.
473. Showcase employee achievements and milestones.
474. Feature employee perspectives and stories.
475. Acknowledge and appreciate employee advocacy efforts.

Customer Appreciation Day

476. Dedicate a day to appreciate your customers.
477. Share personalized messages and shoutouts.
478. Offer exclusive discounts or perks on this day.
479. Create content showcasing customer testimonials.
480. Express gratitude for ongoing customer support.

Customized Merchandise Giveaways

481. Launch giveaways featuring customized merchandise.
482. Collaborate with designers for unique giveaways.
483. Use creative entry requirements for engagement.
484. Showcase winners with their received merchandise.
485. Encourage tagged photos of customers using the merchandise.

Highlight Team Achievements

486. Showcase team accomplishments and milestones.
487. Share behind-the-scenes moments from team activities.
488. Introduce team members through engaging profiles.
489. Express gratitude for the collective efforts of the team.
490. Encourage audience interaction with team-related content.

Virtual Backgrounds and Filters

491. Develop branded virtual backgrounds and filters.
492. Encourage users to incorporate these in their content.
493. Share user-generated content featuring your filters.
494. Promote filters as part of your brand's visual identity.
495. Monitor engagement and usage of virtual elements.

Inclusive Promotions for Holidays

496. Create promotions that resonate with diverse holidays.
497. Highlight cultural significance in holiday promotions.
498. Share diverse perspectives on holiday celebrations.
499. Avoid exclusivity in holiday-related content.
500. Express inclusive wishes for various cultural observances.

These tips cover a wide range of strategies to keep your social media marketing dynamic and engaging. Consistently analyze your performance metrics, adapt to evolving trends, and foster meaningful connections with your audience.

Social media is a dynamic landscape, and staying creative and responsive will contribute to your overall success.

CONCLUSION

In conclusion, "The Social CEO: A Guide to Effective Business Social Media Management" is an essential resource for any business leader looking to leverage the power of social media to drive growth and success. By adopting a strategic and thoughtful approach to social media management, CEOs and other executives can build stronger connections with customers, drive brand awareness, and create meaningful engagement with their target audience.

Throughout this book, we've explored the key elements of effective social media management, including setting clear goals, developing a strategic plan, creating and curating compelling content, engaging with your audience, monitoring and analyzing your results, and expanding your reach through partnerships and advertising. We've also discussed the importance of maintaining a strong brand reputation and having crisis management procedures in place to respond to any negative feedback or backlash.

By following the advice and strategies outlined in this book, you can become a true "Social CEO" - a leader who understands the power of social media and leverages it to drive business success.

---

www.ingramcontent.com/pod-product-compliance
Lightning Source LLC
Chambersburg PA
CBHW070334220526
45467CB00001B/132